THE
ORGANIC
GARDEN

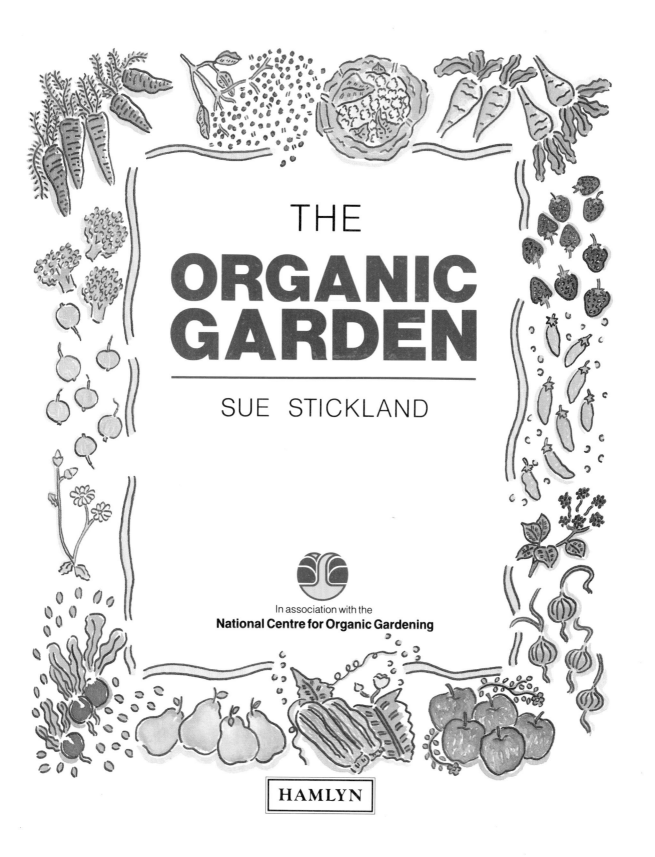

THE
ORGANIC GARDEN

SUE STICKLAND

In association with the
National Centre for Organic Gardening

HAMLYN

Acknowledgements

Front cover illustration by Katherine Greenwood
Photograph of author by courtesy of The Henry Doubleday
Research Association

Colour illustrations by Katherine Greenwood
Line artwork by Vana Haggerty

Photographs: Peter Blackburne-Maze, pages 66, 87, 91; The
Henry Doubleday Research Association, pages 23, 35; Jerry
Harpur, pages 102; Pat Hunt, pages 6, 114, 123; Sue Stickland,
pages 15, 18, 31, 34 (top), 59, 78, 98. All other photographs by
The Hamlyn Publishing Group Limited/Andrew Lawson.

The author would like to thank Mrs Stickland for typing the
original manuscript, Mrs M. Anderson, Janie Harford and Helen
Porter for allowing their gardens to be photographed for this
book, and her colleagues at The Henry Doubleday Research
Association for their help and support.

This edition published in 1989
by the Hamlyn Publishing Group Limited,
a division of the Octopus Publishing Group,
Michelin House,
81 Fulham Road,
London SW3 6RB

ISBN 0 600 56586 6

Printed in Spain by Graficas Estella, Navarra

CONTENTS

INTRODUCTION

Chemicals are not only undesirable in a garden, but completely unnecessary. However, gardening without them is not just a case of throwing away the bottles and ordering a load of manure – though this is not a bad start!

'Organic' gardening is much more than this. It involves an understanding of the garden as a whole – the soil, the weeds, and all the creatures that inhabit it, as well as the crops and ornamental plants. This is not done without effort, but brings its own rewards. A garden need not be just a place to produce food, or riotous colour, or outstanding beauty. It is a place to appreciate the changing seasons – and the different sights, smells and sounds they bring – and poses endless questions about garden life. Answering them makes gardening more interesting, losses more tolerable, and, as we shall see, can lead to a healthy, attractive and productive garden.

Every garden supports an intricate community of creatures, beginning with those that feed on plants, their predators, the higher predators that feed on these predators and so on, up to the small mammals like mice and hedgehogs. Using a chemical to exterminate a particular creature can have far-reaching effects and is almost always self-defeating. Birds may die from eating poisoned caterpillars, and will no longer be there to pick off the next generation of live ones. Meanwhile, other grubs on which the birds also preyed are ruining the crops. Predators are usually fewer in numbers

Opposite: Herbs growing in abundance with iris, verbascum, rue and feathery fennel

and slower to adapt to the change than their prey, and so suffer more from the effects of pesticides.

We ourselves are at the end of this food chain, where the result of all the chemicals sprayed onto the land finally meet – with definite detrimental effects on our health. More and more people feel it is important to know that produce from the garden is free from contaminants.

Just as using one insecticide can eventually reduce the numbers of creatures of all sorts in the garden, so introducing a new plant or a new 'habitat' – like a pond, or simply a dense shrub or a patch of long grass – can have the opposite effect. It will attract other types of insect, which will in turn attract their predators, and so on. All our other gardening activities similarly affect the complex web of garden life, but they do not have to be harmful, and should be regarded as working alongside natural processes rather than battling against them. In some cases, for example, it is possible to tip the ecological balance against a pest by deliberately putting in plants that will encourage its enemies. In general, there should be as much diversity in the garden as possible – flowers as well as many different types of fruit and vegetables; a mixed hedge instead of a row of conifers; climbers planted against bare walls. This will increase the variety of insects and other creatures in the garden, so there will be less chance for any one of them to dominate and become a pest.

One place in the garden that is teeming with unseen life is the soil. This is vital to organic gardening, where it is the soil that feeds the plants rather than soluble chemicals directed to their roots. Most plant foods in the soil come from the return of waste organic matter, which is gradually broken down by bacteria and fungi. This process is happening all the time in nature, but in the garden can be helped along by making compost of all garden and kitchen waste, plus any bought-in organic materials. Compost feeds the bacteria and fungi in the soil, which in turn feed the plants, making available to them a balance of nutrients that promotes healthy growth. It also improves the physical structure of the soil, which is essential, as if the plants are not being force-fed with chemicals on the soil surface they need to make good roots and exploit its full depth. This makes them more stable and less vulnerable to drought.

Much of the success of organic gardening relies on simple *good* gardening. This means always catering for the needs of the plant: never sowing or planting in poor conditions, and finding out whether it needs sun or shade, a rich or a poor soil, moisture or good drainage, shelter from wind or protection from frost. Any one of these factors can improve the appearance or yield of a plant as much

as giving it a dose of fertilizer. Plants grown properly in the right place do not *need* chemical props.

The picture of the organic garden as a paradise of healthy plants and wholesome produce, and a haven for wildlife, is thus not so far from the truth. But it is sadly difficult today to get away from the effects of chemical pollution and the imbalance of the environment caused by factory farming. Manufacturers now realize that words like 'natural' and 'organic' sell products – but these are not always what they seem. Using a dried manure made from the effluent from intensive farms, for example, may bring in unwanted contaminants and is certainly in conflict with the principles behind organic gardening. However, there are a number of products that can be used, in particular those that have the Soil Association symbol, which means that the methods used to produce them are sympathetic towards the environment and that they do not contain undesirable elements. Some details of these products are given in the following chapters, and further advice is always available from one of the organic organizations listed opposite.

ORGANIZATIONS CONCERNED WITH ORGANIC GROWING

HENRY DOUBLEDAY RESEARCH ASSOCIATION
National Centre for Organic Gardening, Ryton-on-Dunsmore,
Coventry CV8 3LG, England

The HDRA has gardens open to the public demonstrating organic growing
and also carries out its own research. Organic products and literatures are
available at the Centre and by mail order. Members receive a quarterly
newsletter.

**HENRY DOUBLEDAY RESEARCH ASSOCIATION OF
AUSTRALIA**
Box 61, Post Office, Australia Square, NSW 20000

THE ORGANIC GROWERS ASSOCIATION
86 Colston Street, Bristol BS1 5BB, England

The OGA is the national organization for commercial organic growers. It is
involved with research, education and the marketing of organic produce.
Together with its fellow organization British Organic Farmers, it publishes
a quarterly journal *New Farmer and Grower*.

THE SOIL ASSOCIATION
86 Colston Street, Bristol BS1 5BB, England

The Soil Association is concerned with all aspects of organic growing,
nutrition, health and ecology. It runs a scheme which guarantees that
organic food and other products which hold its symbol are produced to
rigorous standards. Members receive a quarterly journal.

RODALE RESEARCH CENTER
RD, Box 323, Kutztown, Pennsylvania 18049, USA

Centre for research and education on all aspects of organic growing. Rodale
Press publishes numerous titles on organic gardening, health and nutrition.

I
GETTING TO KNOW THE GARDEN

Planning the garden should thus begin not with the seed and nursery catalogues, but with an assessment of the garden as a whole. What kind of soil has it got? How can this be improved? How much shade and shelter is there? What weeds are established and how can these be dealt with? What pests and diseases are troublesome and how can these be avoided?

The soil

The soil in the garden is far more than an inert material into which plants anchor their roots. It is inhabited by millions of microscopic bacteria and fungi, tiny worms, beetles and other insects, besides the familiar earthworms, slugs and centipedes. This ever changing subterranean community is responsible for the process of decay, as a result of which valuable animal and vegetable waste is returned to the soil. It is a vital part of garden life – influencing both the nutrients that the soil has available to the plants and the physical condition of the soil. These two factors are of

Opposite: Proper care for the soil is the key to healthy carefree growth in this delightful cottage garden

equal importance, as unless the plant roots can move easily through the soil without becoming suffocated or drowned, all its reserves of nutrients will be wasted.

Sandy soils and clay soils

Gardeners have no difficulty in telling whether their soil is light and sandy or heavy clay. Sandy soils are well drained, easy to dig, and warm up quickly in spring; less desirably, however, they lose nutrients and organic matter very quickly. Clay soils are sticky, cold and wet, but to make up for this they hold reserves of plant nutrients. The problems of growing plants on the various types of soils – and their solutions – are quite different.

On a microscopic scale, the difference shows in the size of the mineral particles that make up the soil (see page 12). Nothing can change the soil from clay to sand or vice versa. However, in either case it is possible for the particles to be bound together to give a soil with a good structure. This has spaces that allow roots to penetrate and water to drain, and yet holds good reserves of moisture. Such a well-structured soil can be created first by adding organic matter, and second by gardening the soil in a sympathetic way.

Organic matter

Organic matter can be any bulky animal or vegetable waste, from strawy manure to orange peel. The most common materials available to the gardener are leaves, weeds and plant remains, lawn mowings and domestic waste, together with bought-in materials such as peat, forest bark, hay and straw, farmyard or stable manure and mushroom compost.

Products that have not already undergone some kind of decay are best composted before they are added to the soil. This simply means hastening the natural decay process to produce something more immediately beneficial to plants. Some materials can be composted as they are; others needs to be chopped and/or mixed with other materials. The decomposition is carried out mainly by bacteria and fungi, but worms, insects and other creatures also play a part.

The composting process is a great equalizer, balancing excesses of any one substance that might cause harm if applied to growing plants. It also gives any unwanted chemicals a chance to degrade: ideally, no chemically treated materials should be used, but in practice there are few uncontaminated sources – though some are better than others.

Garden compost

This plays a vital role in the organic garden. It both improves the soil structure and provides a wide range of plant nutrients in small amounts. Its effect is far greater than a simple chemical analysis would indicate.

Any heap of garden debris will decay eventually, and produce valuable material to return to the soil. However, there are various ways of speeding up the process, transforming almost magically the often rather unpleasant ingredients into something that is pleasant to handle and has a clean, earthy smell.

The first requirement is to have a mixture of materials in the heap. It must contain both stemmy things, like old weeds and straw, which provide a lot of carbon, and soft, sappy ones like grass mowings, which provide nitrogen. The decay bacteria need a certain proportion of both these elements in order to work – which is why a pile of sprout stalks left on its own remains a recognizable pile of sprout stalks, and a heap of grass mowings becomes a slimy mass. Moisture is also important – the materials should always be damp but never waterlogged.

Compost activators

Sometimes there is not enough leafy material available, and additional nitrogen has to be added to 'activate' the heaps. Compost activators sold in

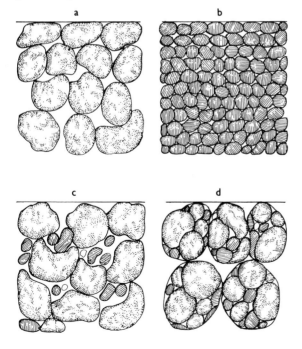

Soil type and soil structure
(a) Sand particles are large so the spaces between them are large also – a sandy soil thus drains quickly. Silt particles are chemically very similar but smaller **(b)** Clay particles are the smallest; they pack closely, retaining water, but waterlogging and lack of air in the soil are problems **(c)** Loams are mixtures of sand, silt and clay particles **(d)** In a well-structured soil, the particles are bound together into 'crumbs'. Small spaces in between hold water, large spaces allow aeration and drainage. This binding effect can be brought about by adding organic matter to the soil

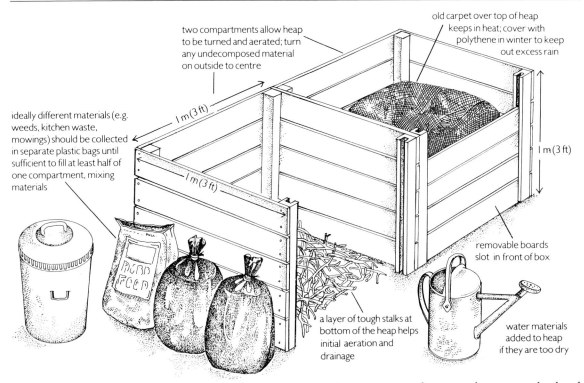

two compartments allow heap to be turned and aerated; turn any undecomposed material on outside to centre

old carpet over top of heap keeps in heat; cover with polythene in winter to keep out excess rain

1 m (3 ft)

1 m (3 ft)

ideally different materials (e.g. weeds, kitchen waste, mowings) should be collected in separate plastic bags until sufficient to fill at least half of one compartment, mixing materials

1 m (3 ft)

removable boards slot in front of box

a layer of tough stalks at bottom of the heap helps initial aeration and drainage

water materials added to heap if they are too dry

A home-made wooden compost box of minimum size

garden shops are usually just chemicals containing nitrogen. The best organic sources are manure (particularly chicken manure), grass mowings, fishmeal, dried blood or urine. Seaweed extracts can also act as activators, though the amount of nitrogen they contain is small. Powders containing dried bacteria and fungi to 'inoculate' the compost, and powdered mixtures of herbs, are often sold specifically as organic compost activators. The exact way in which these act is not easy to determine and there is little scientific evidence to suggest that they work. However, many gardeners do use them – and certainly they do no harm.

Compost shredders

Any coarse material will decay more quickly if it is chopped up or crushed (this gives a larger surface area on which the bacteria can act). There are various mechanical shredders on the market, some hand operated and some driven by electric or petrol motors. Hand-operated ones can be hard work and are not always sturdy enough to take the sort of garden debris that really needs to be shredded – like cabbage stalks. Shears or a spade are often just as good. Motor-driven shredders can be very effective, even shredding woody prunings, but the larger the motor the more expensive the machine, and petrol engines can be noisy.

'Aerobic' compost heaps

One of the most important ways of speeding up composting is to provide air to the heap. This makes it possible for 'aerobic' bacteria to act. They work very fast, and create heat so that temperatures between 49°C (120°F) and 65°C (150°F) can be obtained in the heap, sufficient to kill weed seeds and disease organisms.

The temperature can only be maintained if the heap is insulated, normally by a box or bin, which also keeps it tidy, though even a cover of old carpet will help. In addition, the heap should not be too small, as the outside layers help to insulate the inner ones. A home-made wooden bin (above)

An easy-to-make compost bin known as the New Zealand Box. Compost is covered with a piece of old carpet to keep in the heat

Tumblers can produce compost of a kind quite quickly, even if it is not the ideal clean, friable material that comes from a mature bin, and they have the advantage of being rat–proof and tidy for a small garden.

Worm compost

Another way to deal with a small amount of compost material – particularly kitchen waste – is to set up a worm bin. The worms in this case are 'brandlings' – the thin, reddish worms that are often seen in old compost or manure heaps; they are also used by fishermen, so you can buy them in a fishing shop.

The worms are given a bedding of moist compost, peat, shredded newspaper or leaves, and fed with chopped up vegetable and kitchen waste; they do need a certain amount of protein, so if this is not present in the kitchen waste it may be necessary to add grain or fishmeal. Worms are not happy in acid conditions, so a sprinkling of calcified seaweed (see page 24) may be needed, especially on peat bedding; for the same reason avoid feeding too many fruit peelings. The worms

can be the most effective; many commercial bins are too small and do not insulate the materials, so they never get hot.

There will always be air in a heap when it is first made up, but as decomposition takes place any channels or air pockets become blocked and the slower 'anaerobic' bacteria take over. The only sure way to keep it decomposing quickly and aerobically is to turn the heap. Doing this every week could give good compost in little more than a month in summer! A more practical compromise is to turn it once to create sufficient heat to kill weed seeds and any undesirable organisms, and then allow it to finish decomposing more slowly.

There are 'compost tumblers' on the market – cylindrical bins on spindles - which make it easy to mix and aerate limited amounts of compost. It is important to use the right proportions of different materials, and to fill the tumbler in one go, if possible, rather than adding to it bit by bit.

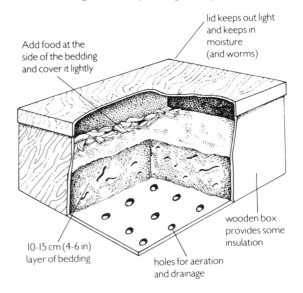

lid keeps out light and keeps in moisture (and worms)

Add food at the side of the bedding and cover it lightly

wooden box provides some insulation

10-15 cm (4-6 in) layer of bedding

holes for aeration and drainage

A worm box can be any size – the number of worms it will accommodate depends on the surface area rather than the depth

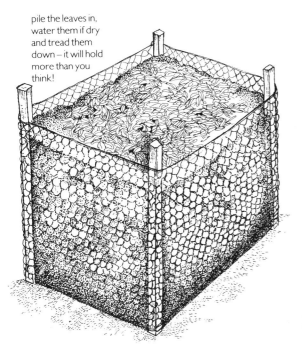

pile the leaves in, water them if dry and tread them down – it will hold more than you think!

A leaf enclosure of wire netting stapled to wooden posts

Leafmould

Leaves that fall from deciduous trees in the wild are gradually taken up by worms and returned to the soil. In the garden, small amounts can be tipped directly into a sheltered shrubbery or onto the compost heap, but they do decay very slowly. Large quantities (and it is worth collecting them, or even asking the local council if they deliver) should be put on a special leaf heap or sealed in dustbin bags. In a year or two they will have formed a dense but rough leafmould, which at least can be used without blowing away. In three years most leaves will have decayed into a fine, crumbly material which is even more useful. It is of little direct nutritional value to the plants but is excellent for improving the soil structure.

A mechanical shredder is an easy way of dealing with tough stems so they decay quickly in the compost heap

work best at temperatures between 13 and 25° C (55 and 77° F) and worm boxes should therefore be kept inside during the winter if possible. This may all seem complicated at first, but experienced worm keepers soon become intuitively aware of their workers' needs!

Worm casts are very rich in nutrients, in a form readily available to plants, and also contain a large number of bacteria; they seem to have a special power for encouraging healthy plant growth. You can remove some compost from the worm box after about two months, when the bedding material has become less recognizable and has increased in volume. This compost will be a mixture of worm castings, bedding and organic waste in various stages of decomposition, and inevitably some live worms and eggs. Alternatively, you can stop feeding and wait until the entire contents of the bin have been converted to worm castings, which will probably take about six months. These castings are more like a fertilizer than compost.

Animal manures

Fresh manure mixed with straw from a cowshed or stable is best composted before use. There are several reasons for this.

First, the high nitrogen content in the manure could harm some plants. Some nitrogen would anyway be lost to the air if the manure were used directly on the garden, whereas if it is properly composted all the nitrogen is taken up by the straw. Conversely, if a mixture containing too much straw is dug into the garden, it will deprive the plants of nitrogen and lead to poor growth.

Second, the composting process will help to break down some, though not all, chemical contaminants. Hormone weedkillers remaining on the straw are a frequent problem, causing distortion and stunting of plants. Tomatoes, beans and sweet peas are particularly susceptible. There may also be contaminants in the manure from chemicals in the animal feed or the drugs used on them. Pig and chicken manure from intensive farms should always be avoided for this reason. Chicken manure from free range hens is very strong but makes an excellent compost activator.

The strawy manure could be stacked, watered if necessary, and covered with plastic to keep it moist and prevent nutrients leaching out in the rain. It should then be left to decompose 'anaerobically' (without oxygen) for six to twelve months, after which it can be used in similar ways to garden compost. Stable manure that contains wood shavings instead of straw must be very well composted and may need extra nitrogen (from any of the compost activators mentioned on page 12) to counteract their effect.

Mushroom compost

Mushroom compost is best avoided unless you have a rare organic source. It consists mainly of straw, broken down with a chemical activator, and large quantities of lime, which can cause problems on alkaline soils (see page 22). It is also likely to contain residues of the persistent chemicals used against the fungus gnats.

Peat and forest bark

Peat contains almost no nutrients but is an excellent material for improving the soil structure. The main drawback is its expense, and it is not always easy to tell whether you are getting value for money because the water content and packed volume of the different types of peat differ widely. Moss peat is usually sold in bales, compressed sometimes to 40 per cent of its actual volume. It is dry and must be watered thoroughly before use. This type of peat should be used in potting mixtures, and is probably the best for garden use too. It is very acid and this makes it useful for increasing the acidity of alkaline soils. Moist black sedge peat is usually sold loose in bags, so it is not always as cheap as the size and weight of the bag make it appear. It is not necessarily so acid but is nevertheless a good soil conditioner.

Forest bark should be pulverized and partially composted before being bagged up for sale. This allows the breakdown of any harmful residues in conifer bark and destroys any fungal diseases. It is available in different grades; coarse chunky grades make very good mulches (page 19), but finely milled grades could be dug in to improve heavy soils. However, the bark does go on decomposing, taking nitrogen from the soil to do so; it is therefore unwise to use it where crops are to be grown. An organic fertilizer containing nitrogen (e.g. fishmeal) can be added if bark is dug in round ornamental plants.

Green manures

Green manures are crops grown specifically for incorporating into the soil. They improve its structure, and although initially they use nutrients to grow, overall there is a net gain to the soil.

Despite the pleasing look of a newly dug patch of garden, it is not generally good organic practice to leave the soil bare. Heavy rain can destroy the structure, weeds start to grow, and it is also a waste of energy and resources. A green manure crop makes use of freely available light and air in manufacturing organic substances that ultimately go into the soil. Some also have bacteria living in nodules on their roots, and these are able to take nitrogen from the air and fix it in the soil.

Green manures can be used to improve ground that is 'resting' or has just been cleared for planting. They can also be grown in temporary spaces on vegetable plots. Here it is the autumn-sown ones like tares or field beans, that are most useful, but sometimes a quick-growing summer type such as mustard can fill a gap. The long-standing green manures with extensive root systems are best for improving poor soils. Details are given below.

Green manures must never be left to become stemmy or go to seed. While they are still young they should either be dug in, chopped off and left on the surface, or mulched (see page 19). Failing that, they can be grown on and cut for composting.

Caring for the soil

Forking and digging are the traditional ways of breaking up the soil, burying or removing weeds and adding organic matter. Although there is still a role for such operations in the organic garden, it is also important not to interfere more than necessary with the structure of the soil and the creatures that inhabit it.

Digging and double digging

Double digging means digging and forking the soil to two spades' depth. It is hard work, but can be valuable for improving drainage, adding organic matter and clearing weedy ground.

Land that has been compacted by machines or continually rotavated often has a hard layer not far

GREEN MANURE CROPS FOR GARDEN USE

Crop	Sowing time	Sowing rate	Time in ground	Use
MUSTARD	March-end August (not winter hardy)	1 oz/6 sq yd (32 g/6 sq m)	4 weeks in mid-summer. Incorporate before flowering when 10–25 cm (4–10 in) high.	A quick-growing gap filler, but a brassica, so should not be grown on ground infected with clubroot. A good weed suppressor.
FENUGREEK	May-early August (not winter hardy)	1 oz/6 sq yd (32 g/6 sq m)	8–10 weeks. Incorporate before flowering when 10–25 cm (4–10 in) high.	A fairly quick summer crop with a good root system. Seed may be difficult to obtain; culinary seed from wholefood shops will usually germinate.
ESSEX RED CLOVER	April-July (winter hardy)	1 oz/10 sq yd (32 g/10 sq m)	2–3 months in summer or leave until spring.	Nitrogen fixer, good for improving spare ground.
WINTER TARES	April-end August (winter hardy)	1 oz/4 sq yd (32 g/4 sq m)	2–3 months in summer or leave until spring.	Nitrogen fixer; good overwintering crop if ground free for August sowing, but does not suppress weeds if sown this late.
GRAZING RYE	Up to mid-October (winter hardy)	1 oz/1 sq yd (32 g/1 sq m)	Incorporate in spring – wait until flower stalks just begin to form to be sure of no regrowth.	Good for late sowing, but can be difficult to incorporate in early spring.

below the surface, causing waterlogging and blocking plant roots. Here, double digging to open up the subsoil is essential before any kind of planting. Incorporating organic matter into the lower layer of soil is a quick way of improving both light and heavy land, but it must be mixed in thoroughly with the soil, not left in a solid layer, or it will not break down easily. Similarly, a surface layer of weeds or turf can be chopped into the lower soil layer. This should be sufficient to kill annual weeds and even surface-rooting perennials, but not those with deep rhizomes (see page 30).

Double digging is thus most appropriate for clearing or improving new ground. The only routine cultivation should be shallow digging to incorporate green manures or compost, and forking to remove perennial weeds or to form a seedbed. And, as the next sections show, even these operations are often unnecessary.

The advice to dig over ground before Christmas really only applies where an early seed bed is needed on a clay soil. In this case the frost helps to break down the clods so that a fine tilth can be

Green manuring – a crop of mustard being dug in while it is still young

A mulch of wood chippings around the rugosa rose 'Frau Dagmar Hartopp'

A peat mulch round a bed of antirrhinums. Always make sure the soil is thoroughly moist before applying any mulch

created. On light soils, or where only a rough surface is needed for planting, any digging should be left until the spring. Whatever the type of soil, never cultivate or even walk on the soil when it is wet, because this destroys the soil structure.

Mulching

Covering the soil with a layer of organic matter – a 'mulch' – is one of the best ways of preserving its structure. It prevents the surface being compacted and eroded by rain and encourages the activity of earthworms. These drag the materials into their burrows, gradually building up the organic content of the soil and making channels that aerate and drain it – a process that occurs everywhere.

Any of the materials mentioned in this chapter can be used for mulching where appropriate – for example, farmyard manure round blackcurrants, compost round cabbages and sprouts, and leaf-mould or peat round small ornamental plants. As the material is not dug in, there is not the same worry about depleting the soil of nitrogen. Materials like organic straw or hay can thus safely be used round fruit, for example, and forest bark or 'woodchips' (shredded tree prunings) round shrubs. Annual green manure crops can be hoed off and left on the soil surface.

Mulching also has many other benefits. It reduces the evaporation of water from the soil and hence the need for watering. It also has an insulating effect, which keeps the soil cooler during hot spells and warmer in cold spells; this is better for plant growth. A mulch thus maintains the status quo of the soil, so it should never be put on when the soil is excessively wet or dry, hot or cold. Late spring and early autumn are usually the best times for mulching.

The last, very significant reason for mulching is to keep down weeds. A few inches of any of the organic mulches described above will successfully prevent annual weeds from germinating. This obviously saves a lot of hoeing, but also means there is less need to tread on the beds and no danger of damaging plant roots near the surface. However, more indestructible mulches are needed to suppress perennial weeds like couch and docks (see page 30).

Fixed-bed and no-dig systems

If the soil structure is so important and mulching so effective, it is natural to ask whether any cultivation is necessary at all. Permanent plantings of fruit, shrubs and perennial flowers can easily be mulched after they are planted and the ground left undisturbed, but it is more difficult to envisage growing vegetables this way.

However, some crops can successfully be grown on good stable soils, even when planted into ground that has not been cultivated for many years; and results should improve markedly as the natural processes of structure formation get to work. It is essential that the whole plot is regularly mulched with organic matter, so 'no-digging' is not such a lazy system as the name suggests. In less than ideal conditions – badly drained land, poor soil or heavy clay – it would be wise to improve the plot before trying no-dig techniques.

An excellent way of growing vegetables, herbs and some soft fruit is in narrow fixed beds separated by permanent paths. The beds can be built up where drainage is bad, and on poor soils it means that the compost can be concentrated on a smaller but highly productive area. It should be possible to reach to the middle of each bed from the path, so all sowing, planting, weeding and harvesting can be carried out without stepping on the soil. On light soils the beds should not need to be dug every year. The beds can be lightly forked if seeds are to be sown, or even mulched with compost.

Sowing and planting

A gardener's influence on producing healthy plants begins here. It is in the initial stages that plants are most vulnerable to weather, pests and diseases, so it is essential to get them off to a good start.

Sowing outdoors

The conditions that seeds need in order to germinate are moisture, air and warmth. A moist, well-structured soil that can easily be raked to a fine tilth is ideal for seed sowing. On cloddy soils, seeds may be lost; fine soils may collapse and cement them in. In poor conditions such as these, sow the seeds into

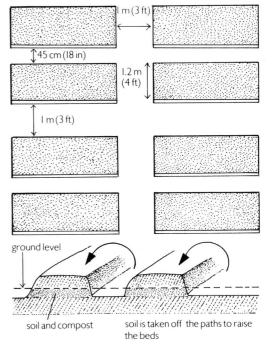

Above: The width of raised or fixed beds should be about 1.2 m (4 ft). Most of the paths need be only just wide enough to walk along, with perhaps a wider one at intervals to take a wheelbarrow *Below*: The beds should be prepared by digging in compost – ideally double digging on poor soils. Where drainage is bad or the soil is thin, the topsoil can be removed from the paths and added to the beds so that they become raised

a layer of peat spread along the seed drill. It is best to sow most seeds in shallow drills: even patches of annual flowers or cutting salads can be made up from a series of shorts rows. This makes weeding much easier. Green manure seeds are usually broadcast and raked into the soil surface. Either way, do not sow too thickly, and thin the seedlings in several stages to their final spacing, so that they are never in competition with each other.

At low temperatures seeds germinate slowly and erratically or not at all: they are more likely to rot or to be eaten by birds, mice or other creatures. Thus there is nothing to be gained by sowing too early. The temperatures needed for the germination of various vegetable seeds are given in Chapter 2. Hardy annual flowers and herbs usually self-seed prolifically so the effect is less noticeable. One further factor, affecting in particular wild flowers and also some herbs and ornamental plants, is their need to experience a cold spell before they will germinate. These seeds should either be sown in autumn or be given an artificial 'winter' by putting them in the freezer for three to six weeks.

Sowing indoors

It is much easier to give seeds ideal conditions if they are sown in pots in the house or greenhouse and planted out later. Although this method is unsuitable for some vegetables (particularly root crops) and some hardy annual flowers and herbs, it is essential for tender crops such as tomatoes and half-hardy bedding plants; it is also a successful way of starting off crops like onions and cabbages, and small quantities of ornamental plants. The disadvantage is the setback they may receive on being planted out. This can be partly avoided by sowing into individual pots or the divided plastic or polystyrene trays now on the market.

The medium used for sowing is critical. It must retain moisture, but not pack down hard in the pot. It must be free from weed seeds and disease spores, and not contain too many nutrients for the tender seedlings to cope with. Garden soil is not suitable on many counts; nor is ordinary garden compost. Organic seed and potting composts

made from peat with various mixtures of dried animal manure, worm casts and organic fertilizers are now more readily obtainable. Alternatively, you could try mixing your own.

Make sure the mixture is damp but not wet before sowing, and cover the pots or trays until the seeds germinate. Several seeds should be sown in each pot or module. Usually the seedlings are thinned later to leave just the strongest, but there are exceptions: onions, for example, give higher yields when 'multisown' (see page 61).

Planting

Always aim to minimize the shock of transplanting. Plants raised indoors should be hardened off by leaving them outside in their pots for a few days beforehand. When possible, choose a dull, calm day for putting in any leafy plants – whether these are vegetables and bedding plants you have raised yourself or container-grown perennial plants bought from a nursery. Water them *before* planting to make sure the root ball is moist. Firm the soil down around the roots gently but firmly when planting, and afterwards water the plant to wash soil into any remaining air spaces.

Bare-rooted trees and shrubs can be put in any time during the autumn and winter months when they are dormant, except when the soil is very wet or frosted. After the ground has been prepared for each plant, dig out a hole that is wide enough to take the fully spread roots and deep enough to make the soil level the same as it was in the nursery – a mark should be visible on the stem or trunk. It can be as damaging to plant too deep as it can to plant shallowly. Shake the tree or bush gently as you fill in the hole to make sure that soil falls among the roots, and firm it well.

Plant food and plant feeding

Plants need a number of different nutrients in order to grow, some in large quantities, others more modestly, and many in only 'trace' amounts. These trace minerals are still vital to the health of the plants – a fact frequently neglected by 'chemical' gardeners. Chemical fertilizers usually contain only one or two of the main plant foods, in a soluble form, and 'force feeding' these in large amounts can discourage plants from taking up other nutrients from the soil.

Two of the main sources of food are air and water, which provide carbon, hydrogen and oxygen (hence the importance of sowing green manure crops to make full use of these free resources). The other major plant foods are nitrogen (N), phosphorus (P) and potassium (K). Nitrogen is the nutrient that encourages the quick growth of leaves and shoots. Fruiting vegetables, like potatoes and tomatoes, and all fruit crops, need most potassium, whereas phosphorus is needed for all new root and shoot growth. All the major nutrients, together with minor and trace elements like calcium, magnesium, manganese, sulphur, iron and copper, occur naturally in most soils from weathering of minerals and the return of organic matter. Nitrogen can also be taken from the air by some bacteria in the soil – in particular those that inhabit nodules on the roots of leguminous plants (the pea and bean family).

Other bacteria and fungi are responsible for the breakdown of the organic matter in the soil to simple, soluble forms that the plant can absorb, and all these micro-organisms thrive and multiply in the conditions provided by an organic garden. In contrast, adding chemical fertilizers can inhibit their action, and the effect on them of chemical fungicides, pesticides and weedkillers can also be harmful.

Soil acidity

The acidity or alkalinity of the soil also has an effect on how available its nutrients are to plants. In a slightly acid soil most nutrients dissolve slowly into the soil water and can thus be taken up by the roots. However, if the soil becomes too acid, nutrients may be washed out altogether or they may remain in the soil water in toxic quantities; in addition phosphorus – one of the main nutrients – becomes unavailable. At the opposite extreme, if the soil becomes too alkaline most of the trace elements become insoluble and are locked into the soil.

The other effect of soil acidity is on the micro-organisms and earthworms in the soil. The bacteria and fungi that break down organic matter become less active as the acidity increases, and earthworms will move out of a very acid soil; thus the valuable effect of these creatures is lost.

It is important to determine the acidity of the soil in your garden. This can be done with one of the simple testing kits on the market. These measure the 'pH' of the soil, in a range from about 4.5 (very acid) to 8.0 (very alkaline). A value of 7.0 is neutral. Most vegetables and fruit grow best on a soil with pH values between 6.0 and 6.5; most ornamentals are tolerant of acid and alkaline soils, but a few will only grow where it is very acid.

A soil can be made less acid by adding lime. The pH test kit should give you an indication of how much is needed. This depends on the soil type. A sandy soil takes less than a heavy clay. If in doubt, add too little rather than too much (overliming can be very harmful), and do it gradually; it is usually sufficient to lime every three or four years. The best forms to use are ground limestone or dolomite, both of which are made slowly available by the soil bacteria; in addition, dolomite contains valuable magnesium. Calcified seaweed is also good for making the soil less acid. Wood ash will do the same, but it is very soluble and its make-up is variable; it is best used on the compost heap.

It is less easy to make an alkaline soil acid: only the constant addition of organic matter (particularly acid peat, where practical) can help.

Organic fertilizers

The breakdown of returned organic matter in the soil is usually sufficient to provide nutrients for most ornamental plants. But some vegetable and fruit crops, where a lot of new growth is made and taken away each year, take considerable quantities of major nutrients from the soil – sometimes during times and at rates at which the natural processes cannot keep up. Nitrogen is the nutrient most likely to be in short supply as it is easily washed out of the soil, and the bacteria that release more act slowly in cold weather. As a result, plant

Comfrey is a valuable garden fertilizer (see page 25)

growth is slow and the older leaves turn pale green, then yellow. The main sign of potassium deficiency is brown scorching along the leaf edges; poor growth and dull, blue–green leaves show a shortage of phosphorus.

Amateur kits that measure nitrogen, phosphorus and potassium in the soil can be unreliable, and where persistant problems occur or when taking over a new garden, a professional analysis would be advisable. (Firms that provide this service are often advertised in gardening magazines; a local agricultural college might also be able to help.) However, even this can be misleading, as it will only measure what is immediately available and the reserves in an organically managed garden can be much greater.

Any deficiencies of nutrients in the soil or extra feed needed for particular plants can be provided by organic fertilizers or natural rock minerals. Organic fertilizers are those of animal or vegetable origin. They are called 'fertilizers' rather than 'manures' because they have no bulk to contribute to the structure of the soil but are concentrated sources of plant nutrients. Nevertheless, unlike their chemical equivalents, they must still be acted upon by soil organisms that convert the nutrients into a form that the plants can absorb. In fast-acting fertilizers, however, this is a quick and easy process. Organic fertilizers also contain a range of trace elements as well as the major nutrients.

ORGANIC FERTILIZERS, GROUND MINERALS AND LIQUID FEEDS

DRY ORGANIC FERTILIZERS

DRIED BLOOD A very quick-acting source of nitrogen.

FISHMEAL A useful source of nitrogen and phosphorus, fairly quick acting.

BONEMEAL Rich in phosphorus and also contains a little nitrogen. Fairly slow acting, depending partly on how finely it is ground.

BLOOD, FISH AND BONE Supplies phosphorus and some nitrogen but scarcely any potassium – any brand listing a %K will almost certainly have it added in chemical form.

HOOF AND HORN Supplies mainly nitrogen; slow action, depending on how finely it is ground.

SEAWEED MEAL One of the few organic fertilizers containing a significant amount of potassium; also supplies nitrogen and a small amount of phosphorus, so is near to being a complete fertilizer like the chemical Growmore.

CALCIFIED SEAWEED Contains a very wide range of minerals, particularly calcium and magnesium, but none in large quantities, though it is said to help release phosphorus and potash locked up in the soil. It is valuable for poor soils needing trace elements and it can also be used instead of lime to increase alkalinity. It is claimed to work as a compost activator, not because it has a high nitrogen content but because its porous particles provide a good breeding ground for bacteria. This also helps its action in the soil.

DRIED ANIMAL MANURES There are several brands of dried animal manure on the market, providing all the nutritional benefits of farmyard manure without the constraints of its bulk. The problem is that some come from intensive farms and contain contaminants (see page 16). If in doubt about a particular product, contact one of the organizations listed on page 9.

WORM CASTS A concentrated and balanced source of plant foods which you can produce at home (see page 14). The same reservations as for manures apply to products in the shops, as the worms may be fed on the output from intensive farms.

GROUND MINERALS

ROCK POTASH From natural rock containing about 10 per cent potassium, ground to a fine dust; some is available fairly quickly, but it will last in the soil for up to five years.

ROCK PHOSPHATE A natural ground rock providing a more lasting source of phosphorus than bonemeal.

DOLOMITE A ground rock similar to limestone, but containing magnesium as well as calcium. Use instead of lime for increasing the alkalinity of the soil, and for correcting magnesium shortage.

GYPSUM A ground rock made up mostly of calcium sulphate, which supplies sulphur to the soil. However, it is most often mixed with dolomite and used as a 'soil conditioner' for clays, as it gradually helps the small clay particles to stick together and let water drain through.

LIQUID FERTILIZERS

SEAWEED SOLUTIONS Like calcified seaweed, liquid seaweed contains a wide range of minerals (the main plant foods and trace elements) but in small quantities. It is very useful as a foliar feed to correct deficiencies and to increase general plant health, especially of seedlings. It does not contain sufficient nutrients to feed plants in pots or high yielding greenhouse crops, though its effects are greater than a simple chemical analysis would indicate. Liquid seaweed also contains plant growth hormones; this supports claims that it helps rooting, gives plant some resistance to pests and diseases, improves fruit set, and extends the storage life of fruit and vegetables.

LIQUID MANURES Proprietary liquid manures are available, or you can make your own by suspending a sack of well-rotted manure in a water butt. These liquids contain significant amounts of the main plant foods (although not as much as most chemical liquid feeds) and a range of trace elements.

COMFREY LIQUID This can be made as described on page 25. It has a high concentration of potassium, and is therefore particularly useful for feeding fruiting crops such as tomatoes and courgettes. It is also the best feed for greenhouse plants in pots and houseplants. It contains concentrations of nutrients of the same order of magnitude as chemical tomato feeds.

Natural rock minerals, finely ground, can also be used in the organic garden. These stay in the soil for several years, slowly releasing nutrients to the plants as they are made available by natural processes. Their main uses are in correcting any lack of basic nutrients on new or previously mismanaged land, and when preparing for long-term plantings of trees and shrubs.

Plants can take in small amounts of food through their leaves as well as their roots, and this will act very quickly where it is needed. Some of the organic liquid feeds that contain a wide range of minerals are thus ideal for foliar feeding – spraying in a dilute form on the leaves – to correct any deficiency.

The most useful organic fertilizers, green manures and liquid feeds are listed opposite. Many of the organic fertilizers can be bought at ordinary garden shops, but seaweed meal, calcified seaweed and worm casts are less easily obtainable, as are the ground minerals. These are available from specialist suppliers – often by mail order, but with the drawback that postage on such heavy items can double the price.

Comfrey

The native species of comfrey, *Symphytum officinalis*, is a perennial plant that grows wild in damp places all over Britain and is a powerful medicinal herb. It is also valuable as a fertilizer in the garden, as its leaves contain amounts of nitrogen and phosphorus comparable to those in farmyard manure and compost, and far more potassium. There is also a vigorous hybrid called Russian comfrey, which has been developed particularly for gardeners and smallholders – its leaves can be cut down up to four times during the growing season and will still grow strongly again. Comfrey is thus a useful quick organic source of potassium, particularly for vegetables like tomatoes and potatoes. The leaves can be dug directly into the soil, laid in potato trenches or used as a mulch – they are readily broken down by bacteria without causing any deficiency of nitrogen. They can also be used to make a liquid feed or added to the compost heap as an activator.

A comfrey patch can therefore be an asset to any garden. Russian comfrey can be bought as plants or as offsets – pieces of root with growing shoots – which can be planted at any time from early spring to late autumn, about 75 cm (30 in) apart. Of course, such a useful fertilizer cannot be produced for nothing. The patch, which should be in a sunny position, takes up valuable growing space, and the plants will need feeding, though they can use any fresh manure – even chicken manure. It will also be a permanent feature, as comfrey is very deep rooting and is not easy to get rid of.

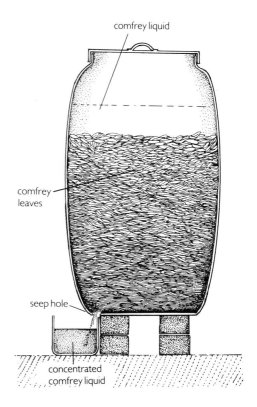

comfrey liquid

comfrey leaves

seep hole

concentrated comfrey liquid

A concentrated comfrey liquid can be made by stuffing freshly cut comfrey leaves into a plastic container – any size from an 18 litre (4 gal) bucket to a water butt. Cover the container and leave them to ferment. After about two weeks, depending on how warm it is, the concentrated black liquid will begin to seep out of a small hole made in the bottom of the container and can be collected. It should be diluted with water (1 : 20) before use

Weeds and weed control

Weeds are undesirable among crops and ornamental plants for several reasons. They make the garden look uncared for, some can harbour specific pests and diseases, and worst of all, they compete for moisture, food and light.

However, weeds are not always out of place. A covering of weeds can act as a green manure, provided that it is dug in before they seed, and in autumn it could protect plants from frost. Some weeds can even be pleasing to look at – a few red poppies or bright green sunspurge in the vegetable patch do no harm; clover and birdsfoot trefoil help the health of a lawn and are as effective as grass at covering the ground, adding a pleasing change of colour and texture. A few weeds are good to eat: chickweed and garlic mustard, for example, go well in a winter salad. Nevertheless, weeds usually need to be removed; in the organic garden, where there will be many different weed species, rather than just a few weedkiller-resistant ones, they make a valuable contribution to the compost heap. Weeds are adapted to surviving in their particular niche, and getting to know their characteristics is the best way to start tackling them.

Annual and biennial weeds

Annual weeds grow from seed, flower and die all in one year. Biennials take two years to do the same, spending their first winter as a low-growing rosette of leaves. The different species all survive by their remarkable ability to produce seed under almost any conditions, and by the ability of the seed to remain viable in the soil for a long period – up to forty years or more in some cases. Large plants left in a fertile vegetable patch can produce many thousands of seeds, but even a tiny stunted plant in a path will produce a few, often before you have even noticed it is there.

Not all the seeds of a plant will germinate at once. Some have a built-in mechanism which

Opposite: The poppies allowed to grow in this path please the eye and do no harm

keeps them dormant in the soil for a certain period or until particular outside conditions are right. For example, knotgrass seeds must have experienced winter cold before they will germinate, whereas others need midsummer temperatures. However, some weeds, like groundsel and annual meadow grass, grow and seed readily from early spring to late autumn. Thus the observant gardener can follow the seasons as much from the emergence of weeds as from the garden flowers – and knows when to be on guard.

Perennial weeds

Perennial weeds are those that live for more than two years, and often do so for much longer. They rely on underground roots or bulbs to bring them through winter cold or summer drought. They often spread by means of these underground parts, though most do also produce seeds.

Weeds such as dandelion and docks have one long tap root in which food for the plant is stored. These deep roots can also bring up water and minerals from well below the soil surface. If the leaves are cut off, the root simply pushes up new ones. If the roots are cut up, the pieces will often produce new plants.

Weeds with very deep, branching roots like creeping thistle and bindweed are even more persistent: they can survive equally well among closely growing perennial plants and in cultivated ground. Others develop a mat of creeping stems, spreading rapidly above or just below ground, like couch, creeping buttercup and ground elder. Sections of the stem can develop new plants, so again they easily survive in cultivated ground.

Weeds such as daisies, plantain, yarrow and clover are rarely a problem on the vegetable patch, but survive well in lawns because their low, compact growth of leaves and short flowering stems escape the mower blades.

Controlling weeds

Annual weeds can be killed simply by chopping them down or hoeing them off, because the roots

COMMON GARDEN WEEDS

ANNUAL MEADOW GRASS	Shallow, fibrous roots forming dense clumps; not easy to hoe; seeds and grows almost all year round; mulching is the best control.
BINDWEED	Deep, thin but persistent roots which get among the roots of perennial crops and flowers; the shoots twine up their stems to the light and are almost impossible to pull away without damage; clearing by mulching with carpet or black plastic for at least a whole growing season is the best control. It will often push through any planting holes in the mulch.
BULBOUS BUTTERCUP	Tubers are easy to fork up, but any bits cut away will resprout. Needs more than one growing season to kill by mulching.
CHICKWEED	An annual weed which seeds prolifically and grows through the winter; easily hoed in summer but a problem in winter salad crops. Try to get a clear seed bed before sowing.
CREEPING BUTTERCUP	Creeping stems just above ground. Can be forked out but this is difficult on the heavy, wet land which it prefers. Can easily be mulched out.
CREEPING THISTLE	Deep, brittle, underground storage roots, bits of which will produce new plants. Best mulched out with one of the long-lasting mulches.
COUCH GRASS	Shallow white underground rhizomes which can produce a dense mat. Clear by double digging, continual rotavating in a dry spell or a long-lasting mulch.
DANDELION	Large tap root, even small pieces left in the ground will regrow; can be forked out – eventually. Do not let it seed.
DOCK	As for dandelion, although it may be less inclined to grow if only the very end of the root is left in the ground.
GROUND ELDER	Shallow roots forming a mat. Control as couch grass.
GROUNDSEL	An annual that seeds abundantly and grows all year round, but easy to hoe or pull out.
HAIRY BITTERCRESS	A small annual often brought in on plants in pots – exploding pods disperse seeds, resulting in many widely spread seedlings; control by constant hoeing and weeding to catch them before they flower.
HORSETAIL	Deep, penetrating, black rhizomes; control as for bindweed or creeping thistle.
LESSER CELANDINE	Grows in early spring; leaves die down in summer. Produces a cluster of bulbils just below the surface, each of which will regrow – do not try to pull the plant up or rotavate. Dig the root ball out with the soil round it or use mulch from very early spring to summer.
NETTLE	Deep branching yellow roots and horizontal rhizomes. Dig them out or use a long-lasting mulch. Fairly easily worn out by continual cutting.
OXALIS	Bulbils – control as for lesser celandine, although mulch will be needed for more than one whole growing season.
SHEPHERD'S PURSE	Seeds prolifically and explosively; control as hairy bittercress.

do not generate new growth. There are hoes adapted for working both between plants and on larger open patches, as the illustration shows; they can make a job quick and easy – and even pleasurable. Hoeing is best carried out while the weeds are still small, on a day when the soil is dry so that they do not re-root. Hoe shallowly, as deep hoeing may damage plant roots and brings weed seeds to the surface, where they can germinate.

Annual weeds will also be killed by digging or rotavating them into the soil, though some densely matted ones, such as annual meadow grass, may persist in wet conditions. If the weeds have gone to seed or are old and stemmy, it is better to pull them up and put them on the compost heap.

Flame-weeding is a method widely used by commercial organic growers to deal with annual weeds. Burners fuelled by liquid butane or propane are passed quickly over the weed seedlings: they are not burnt, just singed enough to break down their cell structure, and there is little heating of the soil. This method particularly benefits slow-germinating crops such as carrots, where the flame-weeder can be passed over the seed bed just before the crop seedlings emerge. There are small

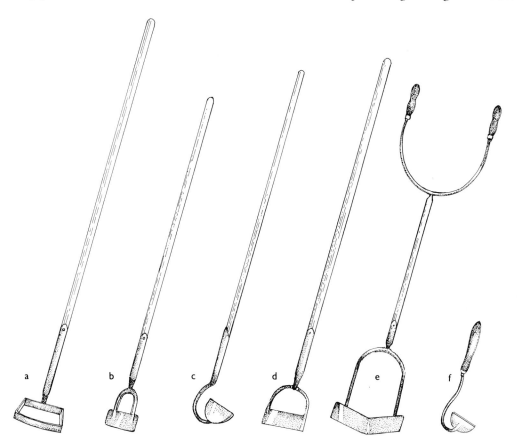

Different types of hoe
(a) Reciprocating hoe has a square section blade which pivots back and forth cutting both ways, so use with a push-pull action (b) Narrow Dutch hoe for between vegetable rows, etc. (c) Draw hoe is pulled rather than pushed; usually used for earthing up and drawing a drill (d) Dutch hoe or 'push hoe' for general garden use (e) Lincolnshire Longhorn has a wide blade for covering large bare areas (f) Onion hoe for weeding in any small space

gas-fuelled flame-weeders suitable for the gardener on the market – for example, ones with a lance attached to a single cylinder, used almost like a sprayer. Their best use is for dealing with weeds on paths, leaving no residue of chemicals, but there is no reason why they should not be used carefully elsewhere if necessary.

The main defence against annual weeds in the organic garden is mulching (see pages 19–20). A thick layer of organic materials – compost, leafmould, bark, hay or grass mowings – is usually sufficient to keep weeds from germinating, and any that do grow have their roots in loose materials and are easy to pull out.

Perennial weeds are not so easy to deal with. Regular hoeing weakens them, as they are continually using their stored reserves to make new leaves, but it may be several years before they give up. Tap-rooted weeds can be dug or forked out – but most will regenerate from any little piece left behind (dandelion and horseradish are notorious) and rotavating a patch containing such weeds will only make the problem worse.

Weeds like couch, with shallow, creeping

MULCHES FOR CONTROLLING PERENNIAL WEEDS

Material	Method	Uses
BLACK PLASTIC	This can be bought in various thicknesses (measured in microns μ or by the 'gauge'). Thicker plastics are more expensive but last longer. 150 gauge (38 μ) is very thin – like a cheap dustbin bag – but will last for one growing season. Thick 300 gauge could be reused if no planting holes are made in it. Hold it down by burying the edges in the soil.	Very good for land clearance. Almost anything can be planted through it – from smaller lettuces and alpines to shrubs. 'Mulching mats' can be cut for isolated trees and shrubs (see opposite). The plastic can be covered in gravel, coarse bark or woodchips for an attractive finish. Water through planting holes or lay seephose beneath the plastic.
BLACK 'WOVEN' PLASTIC	A material often marketed as 'ground cover', which is dense enough to keep down weeds but which will let water through. Bury edges in soil to secure it.	Used for fairly permanent plantings – soft fruit, for example – and where pots of plants are to stand outside.
CARPET	Old carpet will keep down weeds for at least a growing season – the heavier wool and hessian-backed ones are best! Hold down with small pegs of stiff wire.	Most useful for ground clearance. Can also be used on paths, covered with bark or woodchips for appearance.
CARDBOARD	Use flattened cardboard boxes – the bigger the better – and overlap the edges to prevent weeds creeping through. Keep down with bricks or cover with old wet straw or hay.	Most useful for ground clearance, but can be used round fruit bushes or trees, or perennial vegetable crops, if appearance is not important.
NEWSPAPER	A thickness of at least one whole newspaper is needed to keep down weeds. Hold by covering with old straw or hay, or woodchips.	Could be used round fruit, as above, round widely spaced vegetables, or on paths between beds.
COMPRESSED PEAT PAPER	Hold down by burying edges in the soil or with planks. Barely lasts a growing season before rotting into the soil (especially at points where it is held down).	Intended for use with any vegetable crops, but not suitable for very small transplants. Appearance not bad at first but brown colour becomes bleached, which can keep soil cold.

rhizomes, can sometimes be forked out on good light soil, but all too often they have already formed an inpenetrable mat. In this case the rhizomes can either be buried completely at a depth of 15 cm (6 in) or more by double digging, or they can be exhausted by continual rotavation: choose a dry period in summer, rotavate to chop up the rhizomes, let them resprout and rotavate again – and repeat the process until there is no further growth; intervals between rotavating will be about three weeks. However, the method is unlikely to be successful for weeds with deep branched roots.

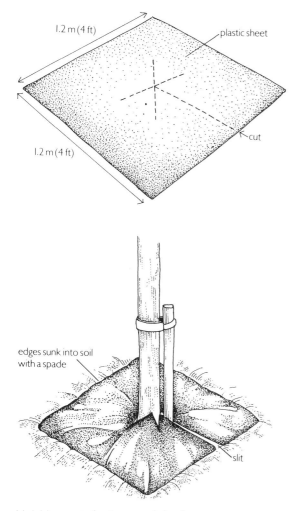

Mulching mats for trees and shrubs

This recently planted hedge has a double mulch of wood chippings over black plastic – enough to cope with most perennial weeds

A list of some common problem garden weeds and how to deal with them is given on page 28. As this shows, it is almost impossible to get rid of most perennial weeds from among established plants – the problem must be tackled *before* planting. They must be removed by cultivation, or preferably by excluding light from them for a whole growing season using a long-lasting mulch. Some suggestions of suitable materials and their use are given opposite. Some come very cheaply – and old carpet on its way to the dump is one of the easiest to use and most effective for clearing a spare patch of land. On the other hand, even the most delicate plants can succeed in weedy ground if they are planted through a thin black plastic sheet; this can be completely diguised with a covering of gravel, wood chips or a coarse grade of bark.

Pest and disease control

Pests and diseases are less of a problem in the organic garden, as healthy plants grown in compost-fed soil are far more resistant to attack. In addition, growing a mixture of different plants means there should be plenty of natural predators and beneficial organisms to help keep any outbreaks in check. However, this does not mean that pests and diseases can be forgotten. On the contrary, you should be continually on the watch for trouble, so that it can be caught in the early stages and avoided in future. As with weeds, the first line of defence is to identify the enemy, and the second is to look for a weak link in its life cycle where control would be possible. Some creatures are obvious villains, but there are many more that are helpful, and these are all too often destroyed in mistake for, or along with, a pest.

Pests

From the plant's point of view, rather than the entomologist's, there are three main types of pest: leaf- and fruit-eating pests, sap-sucking pests, and root-eating soil pests; plus the larger pests like rabbits and mice that are easy to identify, if not to deter!

The first group includes caterpillars, leaf miners, fleabeetles, capsid bugs, sawfly larvae, slugs and snails. Many of these are fairly specific in their diet, and are discussed in more detail in the following chapters. Leaf-eaters like caterpillars can often simply be removed by hand if there are only a few. The sort of grubs which feed inside fruit or pea pods are more difficult to deal with, but knowing their life cycle sometimes means they can be caught before they hide.

Slugs and snails are ubiquitous, and are often the most troublesome pests in the organic garden, feeding on the young shoots and leaves of almost any plant. Warm, moist conditions are their ideal, and you will find most if you go out on a damp summer night with a torch to hunt them down. They dislike dry weather because they lose water very easily, particularly in making the slimy mucus on which they glide – hence the old remedy of putting dry peat or ashes around plants for their protection. This is rarely a sufficient deterrent, however; nor are traps of sticky liquid, which unfortunately catch beneficial insects too. The only sure thing that will keep slugs away from young plants is a solid barrier like that of the bottle cloches (see below).

The second group of pests includes all the aphids (greenfly, blackfly and mealy cabbage aphid, for example), froghoppers, spider mites and scale insects. The various aphids often have very specific host plants, or alternate between two entirely different plants, but the general effect that they produce is the same. They feed by puncturing the plant tissue and sucking out the sap, which itself weakens the plant and causes the familiar symptoms of curled leaves and distorted shoots. It has other detrimental effects as well. All parts of the plant become covered in a sticky residue or 'honeydew' excreted by the aphids, which itself rapidly becomes infected with a unsightly black fungus known as sooty mould. Less obvious, but more· serious, is that by piercing into the plant tissues all sap-sucking insects can spread virus diseases from one plant to another.

Aphids occur in large colonies, but they have

Left: Plastic bottles can be used to protect young plants against slugs. Cut off the bottom of the bottle, remove the cap and press it firmly into the ground
Right: Similar collars cut from the bottles can be used to protect the stems of larger plants against cutworms

many enemies, and it is often worth letting these have a chance to reduce the numbers. Sometimes aphid colonies can be squashed without causing damage to the plant or the first infected leaves can be removed, but this is difficult on young plants. As a last resort, many of the plant-based sprays listed on page 36 are effective against aphids.

Soil pests do not usually become obvious until the first signs of trouble appear – wilting plants or holes in root vegetables, for example. These pests include leatherjackets, cutworms, vine weevils, wireworms, chafer bug larvae, millepedes, some slugs and the grubs of various flies like the carrot fly, onion fly and cabbage root fly.

The life cycles of these fly grubs have been well researched and show that there are effective ways of avoiding damage (see pages 51–2). The other soil pests are less selective in their choice of food. Most will nibble away at fibrous roots or make holes in bulbs or root crops. A few come to the surface at night and feed on the plant stems: cutworms and leatherjackets are notorious for this, cutting right through the stems at ground level and leaving the sad, wilted plant lying on the soil. Sometimes digging up the roots immediately will reveal the culprit.

Leatherjackets and wireworms are commonly a problem in ground brought into cultivation from grass, and on such plots it would be wise to delay using no–dig techniques for a while: digging and forking expose all soil pests to the frost and to their natural enemies, the birds. Soil pests are not usually a problem among established plants with good root systems.

Diseases

Plant diseases can be caused by fungi, bacteria or viruses. Fungi and bacteria cause the various moulds, mildews and spots that affect leaves, the rots and cankers that affect fruit and bulbs, and the galls like clubroot disease of brassicas. Viruses can affect any plant, though some are more prone to trouble than others. Typical virus symptoms are mottled and distorted leaves and flowers, stunted growth and poor yields.

For all these diseases, prevention is better than attempting a cure, for they can spread rapidly among crops and controlling them – even using chemicals – is difficult. A virus-infected plant, for example, can only be pulled up and burned. Giving plants the right growing conditions goes a long way towards avoiding diseases. In fact symptoms not unlike those of a disease can be caused just by poor conditions – lack of water, waterlogging, temperatures that are too hot or too cold, and mineral deficiencies (see pages 23–5) all make the plants look sickly, and can all be avoided. Overcrowding and lack of garden hygiene are other common causes of plant disease.

Beneficial insects and other creatures

One of the most familiar garden friends must be the ladybird. The adults feed on a number of pests, such as scale insects, mealybugs and, most commonly, aphids; their larvae are even more voracious, each eating perhaps several hundred aphids during its three-week life. Ladybirds hibernate in dry, sheltered spots like crevices in trees and walls, hollow plant stems, and under loose boards in a garden shed. Sometimes a few dozen will be found in a favoured spot and this will be used year after year – a point to be remembered when tidying up in the garden.

Ladybirds are just one of the many insects that prey on aphids. Hoverflies are in fact rather better predators, as not only do their larvae eat large numbers of aphids but the adults are much more efficient about laying their eggs, choosing places close to large aphid colonies. Hoverflies can be attracted to the garden by simple colourful flowers, from which they can easily extract nectar and pollen. Among their favourites are the yellow and white poached egg plant (*Limnanthes*), pot marigolds (*Calendula*), yarrow (*Achillea*), the annual convolvulus (*Convolvulus tricolor*) and baby blue eyes (*Nemophila*). Larvae of the delicate green lacewing are also active aphid predators.

One problem with relying on natural enemies to keep aphids under control is the delay between the colonies appearing on garden plants and the

Shasta daisy (top) and *Convolvulus tricolor* (above) both attract beneficial hoverflies to the garden

predators mustering strength, especially early in the year. For new young plants this can be devastating, and other methods of control are justified (see page 36). Nettle aphids are among the first to appear in spring, and can build up the strength of the predators ready for moving onto your crops – so a patch of nettles in the garden *can* be useful.

The beneficial insect most trodden on without trial is probably the ground beetle. Nearly all species are predators on a number of pests – notably slugs and snails, caterpillars and the larval stages of the cabbage root fly. The beetles feed mainly at night, and during the day appreciate the cover of logs, stones and low, dense vegetation or organic matter on the soil – so mulching or growing a green manure crop has the additional benefit of encouraging these creatures.

Ladybirds, hoverflies and ground beetles are the friendly insects you are most likely to encounter in the garden, but a close inspection would reveal a whole lot more – like the ichneumons, which are parasites of caterpillars, and the black-kneed capsid bugs, which keep fruit tree red spider mites in check – together with a host of antagonistic micro-organisms that help to control diseases.

Then there are the larger predators. Frogs, toads, slow-worms and hedgehogs, for example, all consume significant amounts of slugs. The first three can be encouraged into the garden by creating a small informal pond and wet grassy area; hedgehogs, on the other hand, like to shelter in dry leaves beneath dense hedges or shrubs.

Birds cause mixed emotions: few would deny the pleasure they bring – except when sparrows are tearing the first spring crocus flowers or eating young peas, and blackbirds regard the strawber-ries as their own! On the whole, however, the good that they do far outweighs the bad. The regular loud tapping as a song thrush cracks a snail is one reminder of this, as is the beady-eyed robin picking up small soil pests as you dig. Bluetits are also very useful. They eat large numbers of overwintering aphids and codling moth larvae. The best approach is to encourage birds to the garden, with food and suitable roosting and nesting sites – but first cover up vulnerable crops with netting.

While many birds do eat pests, their diets are varied and will also include beneficial insects. However, studies have shown that birds eat *more* of the most *abundant* types of insects, until these are reduced in number. The same seems likely to be true of bats, who include aphids, cutworm moths, craneflies and other pests in their diet, and wasps, whose larvae are often fed on various moth and sawfly caterpillars. Thus the feeding habits of these creatures tend to suppress pest outbreaks as soon as their numbers begin to build up.

Preventing pest and disease attacks

Prevention can begin even before new plants reach the garden. In choosing varieties of fruit, flowers and vegetables, look out for those that show resistance towards certain pests and diseases. Many new soft fruit and some new vegetable varieties have been bred to have considerable disease resistance and are well worth making an effort to obtain.

Always buy seeds, bulbs and plants from a reliable source. Fruit should if possible come from a nursery whose stock is certified as 'virus free' (see page 69). Inspect bought-in plants of any kind for signs of pests or disease: downy mildew on bedding plants, basal rot of bulbs, and scale insects on evergreen shrubs, for example. Be wary of accepting plants from the gardens of neighbours or friends: the soil on the roots of any plant could introduce clubroot, and even cuttings can carry virus diseases.

A gardener needs to have a feel for the changing seasons, watching not only the calendar but also the growth of plants in the garden and elsewhere, for the calendar is not a wholly reliable guide. Never sow or plant before conditions are right, because plants that are struggling to get established are the most vulnerable. For some vegetables, the

Hedgehogs should be welcomed to the organic garden as they consume significant quantities of slugs

PLANT-BASED INSECTICIDES

Type	Source	Use
DERRIS	Made from the roots of a tropical plant: 'rotenone' is the active natural ingredient. Available as a liquid and a dust. Harmless to humans and other mammals, bees and hoverflies, but can kill fish, ladybirds, lacewings and some capsids.	Use liquid against aphids, some weevils and small caterpillars, and dust against fleabeetle and red spider.
PYRETHRUM	Made from an African flower in the chrysanthemum family. Available as a liquid or a dust. Harmless to humans and other mammals, but harmful to bees and some ladybirds.	Use against aphids, small caterpillars and fleabeetles.
DERRIS/PYRETHRUM MIXED	Available as a liquid and dust.	Enhances the effectiveness of both insecticides.
QUASSIA	Taken from the bark of a tropical tree. Available as chips, which must be boiled with water. Harmless to humans, other mammals, and to bees and many other beneficial insects.	Useful against small caterpillars and sawflies.
NICOTINE	Made from the type of plants that produce tobacco. Very poisonous to humans, all other mammals and bees, but harmless to ladybirds, hoverflies, lacewings and many beneficial orchard species. Wear rubber gloves when spraying and do not eat sprayed produce for forty-eight hours afterwards.	Most powerful of this type of insecticide. Because it is so poisonous use only as a last resort. Kills aphids, scale insects, mealy bugs, pea and bean weevils, most caterpillars.
INSECTIDAL SOAP	A liquid soap made from naturally occurring fatty acids. Many soaps have insectidal properties but this formulation is particularly effective. Harmless to humans and other mammals, and to bees and many other beneficial insects. Traditional soft soap, used as a wetting agent with other organic sprays, has some insecticidal action; so do household soaps and detergents, but these may damage plants.	Use against aphids, whitefly, spider mites, mealy bugs, scale insects, slug worms and thrips.

BIOLOGICAL CONTROLS

Type	Source	Use
BACILLUS THURINGIENSIS	Caterpillar killers that contains the spores of this naturally occurring bacterium are completely harmless to all other creatures – the spores are activated only in the caterpillar's gut and they are quickly destroyed by sunlight. Sold as a powder in sealed sachets, to be made up into a liquid.	Kills most butterfly and moth caterpillars, especially if they are still small, but not those of sawflies.
TRICHODERMA PELLETS	The fungus *Trichoderma viride* has an antagonistic effect against certain tree disease organisms. Pellets containing the fungus are inserted into small holes drilled into the trunk.	Effective against silver leaf disease of fruit trees; has also been tried against Dutch elm disease and honey fungus.
TRICHODERMA POWDER	*Trichoderma viride* is also available in a wettable powder which can be mixed into a paste for the treatment of tree wounds, helping to prevent fungal attacks.	Use for all large pruning cuts and wounds – but they must be treated on the day that the cuts were made.

SLUG CONTROL

Type	Source	Use
ALUMINIUM SULPHATE SLUG KILLERS	These are not a bait but act by upsetting the ability of slugs to produce mucus. Although they are NOT organic they do not build up in the food chain. Harmless to humans and other mammals, and to earthworms. Available as granules which can be sprinkled on the soil or made into a liquid; can cause damage if it touches young seedlings.	May reduce slug numbers but not usually effective enough to protect young plants.

HOME-MADE FUNGICIDES

Type	Source	Use
HOME-MADE FUNGICIDES	Reliable organic fungicides are almost impossible to find. If desperate, use a sulphur-based one rather than any of the modern chemicals, some of which are particularly harmful to worms and other beneficial creatures. The following home-made sprays are also worth trying:	
URINE	Synthetic urea is used by commercial fruit growers. Use neat urine on bare trees in spring before buds open and on fallen leaves in autumn. Dilute 1:4 on foliage.	Try against apple and pear scab, and mildew of all fruit.
ELDER LEAF SPRAY	Simmer 450 g (1 lb) of elder leaves in 3.5 l (6 pt) of water for half an hour and strain. Mix with soft soap before spraying. Cyanins may be the active natural ingredient.	Try against any mildew on vegetables or ornamental plants.
RHUBARB LEAF SPRAY	Make as for elder leaf spray – oxalic acid may be the active natural ingredient.	As for elder leaf spray.

sowing and planting dates during the growing season can be planned to miss the worse pest and disease attacks.

Garden hygiene is one of the most important factors in controlling pests and disease. All infected material should be immediately gathered up: rose leaves with black spot, rotting cabbage stumps, and apples with holes in them, for example. Good composting – where the heap heats up – destroys many disease organisms, but there is no reliable information about which of them survive. If in doubt, put infected material on the bonfire rather than the compost heap.

Crop remains left on vegetable plots should also be removed as soon as possible, so that a clean start can be made in the spring; carrot fly, for example, could overwinter on old carrots left in the ground and reinfect the new crop. The build-up of soil pests and diseases in vegetable plots can also be avoided by the rotation of crops around the plots from year to year (see page 43). Regular pruning of fruit trees and bushes helps disease control by removing infected wood and preventing over-crowding.

Apart from this, clearing up in the garden should be a compromise between tidiness and the needs of garden life – friends and foes. As they die down, flowers provide seeds for birds and dry stems shelter overwintering ladybirds. Large stones, logs, and other debris may harbour some slugs, but will also provide shelter for beneficial ground beetles and centipedes.

Most gardeners use netting to protect fruit and put up fences that are rabbit proof, but the idea need not stop here. Physical barriers can be used against other, much smaller pests. Where they can be made to work, these are ideal methods of control because they do not upset the ecology of the garden. The various pests that can be deterred in this way include carrot fly, cabbage root fly, fleabeetle, cutworms, cabbage caterpillars and codling moth. Details are given in Chapters 2 to 4.

Organic pesticides and fungicides

The answer to most pest and disease problems in the organic garden thus lies in understanding them and trying to avoid trouble – which is much more interesting than spraying everything, as well as much safer. However, there are times when an attack threatens to destroy a crop or kill a plant completely and it is then that organic pesticides and fungicides are useful (see opposite). These are acceptable because they are all naturally occurring substances and, used properly, do least harm to beneficial insects and other creatures. They cannot cause any damage to plants. They also break down quickly into harmless products so there is no danger of their persisting on edible crops or passing up the food chain.

2
THE
VEGETABLE
GARDEN

Vegetables are important to most organic gardeners. Understandably, most wish to avoid the chemicals in shop-bought produce. The real taste of home-grown crops, the exciting choice of varieties and the satisfaction of producing them means that the space in a small garden is all too quickly filled.

It is not necessary to grow vegetables in regimented, widely spaced rows as on a conventional allotment. Some will climb up fences, others can be sown in patches in odd corners, while a few are quite decorative enough for a place in the flower border. Growing the main crops in narrow fixed beds (see page 20) means that they can be placed much closer together. Crops can sometimes be mixed, by putting a quick-growing one in the spaces between a slow one, or growing a short one beneath one that is tall. Salad crops, annual herbs or edible flowers can often provide an edging.

This mixed planting looks attractive, and not only does it save space but it also encourages a diversity of insects and micro-organisms. In such an environment it is difficult for one pest or disease to take over and cause a severe attack.

Growing conditions

Most vegetables grow best in a situation that is sunny and open but not windswept. Ideally, the soil should be fertile but well drained, and preferably slightly acid. It is important to work towards this ideal, as vegetables grown in bad conditions will not only give a poor yield but will also be susceptible to attack by pests and diseases that may then spread to other plants in the garden. Improving the physical conditions does as much to increase yields as would adding a chemical fertilizer.

One of the worst places to grow vegetables is near large trees, which not only cast shade but also take moisture and nutrients from the soil; the drips from their branches also produce the sort of atmosphere in which fungal diseases thrive. However, there are ways of improving the conditions in most other sites so that at least certain vegetables can be successfully grown.

Opposite: Marigolds, which attract hoverflies, courgettes and a bed of carrots surrounded by their carrot fly barrier (see page 54)

SUMMER SOWN CROPS FOR SHADY SPOTS	
LETTUCE	ROCKET
LANDCRESS	SPINACH
PEAS	CHINESE GREENS
RADISH	(some)

CROPS FOR HOT SUNNY BORDERS	
TOMATOES	PEPPERS
SWEETCORN	AUBERGINES
COURGETTES	

Sunshine

Shaded areas are really best used for compost bins or ornamental plants. However, there are vegetables that will tolerate light shade. Jerusalem artichokes, for example, will grow well provided the soil is moist and fertile. Similar conditions suit summer sowings of some quick-maturing salad crops, which would tend to bolt quickly in a hotter position.

Borders against hot, sunny walls, on the other hand, are best for tender crops such as tomatoes and sweetcorn. The more exotic ones – peppers and aubergines, for example – may also fruit in good summers, though they are best grown under cloches. Choose varieties carefully, as some of the latest ones are better suited to cooler climates. Keep all crops in such positions well watered and mulched.

Out in the main vegetable patch remember that tall crops – particularly peas and beans – will cause shading. Running rows from north to south rather than from east to west minimizes the effect. Alternatively, keep the tallest crops to the north of the plot, or use the shading effect to your advantage to grow summer lettuce or one of the other 'shady spot' crops.

Wind

Apart from the obvious effects of wind, such as listing bean poles and uprooted sprouts, the yield of some vegetable crops can be reduced by as much as a third in an exposed place. Insects are less inclined to visit the flowers of crops like runner beans and courgettes, which need to be pollinated before they can produce fruit; tall peas and beans will not climb to their full extent; and the buttons on Brussels sprout plants become loose and shabby.

The worst of these effects can be avoided by providing a windbreak. Walls and fences that stop the wind completely are not usually the best answer, as they can cause turbulence in other places in the garden, and in very sheltered spots diseases such as mildew are more likely to take hold in humid weather. Windbreaks that are only half solid are much more satisfactory – slatted fencing, a suitable hedge, or some of the temporary windbreak netting now on the market. Most of the temporary materials will last for about three years if they are properly erected. They should be attached to wooden posts with battening and kept taut. Windbreaks like this are effective over a distance of about six times their height.

Soil

There is no getting away from the fact that having a fertile soil is important for producing good vegetables, and that the initial preparation of the soil is more important than any subsequent additions of fertilizers. The depth of good soil is also important – most noticeably for producing root crops such as carrots and parsnips, though all

CROPS FOR DAMP CONDITIONS	
CELERY	CORN SALAD
CELERIAC	LANDCRESS
CHICORY	LEEKS

crops will benefit if they can make deep roots; watering then becomes less necessary.

The structure of both heavy clays and light, sandy soils should be improved by gradually adding bulky organic matter, usually compost or well-rotted manure (see pages 12–17), and on thin soils this should be worked into the subsoil. Breaking up the subsoil will also go a long way towards improving drainage. No vegetables grow well on a waterlogged soil, but there are a few that tolerate damp conditions, so any permanently moist places should be used for these.

Organic matter is also the answer to water retention on very free-draining soils. Few vegetables grow well in dry conditions; New Zealand spinach and claytonia are perhaps the only two worth trying.

The ideal soil acidity (pH) for vegetable growing is 6.5, but most do well in the range 5.5–7.0. It is advisable to check the pH of your vegetable patch (see page 22), and not to spread lime automatically, as is sometimes recommended.

Preparing the ground for individual crops

Cabbages, sprouts and other leafy brassicas benefit greatly from the addition of farmyard manure or compost, both worked into the ground and used as a mulch (the manure must be well composted in the former case). This helps them to produce a lot of growth over the long period that they are in the ground. In addition, they need an alkaline soil; this helps to prevent clubroot, which is the most damaging disease of brassicas.

Potatoes will also show an increased yield in well-manured or composted ground, though they can be used to 'break in' heavy soil on a new plot and will give a reasonable crop. A slightly acid soil in this case helps to prevent scab disease.

Root crops, on the other hand, grow too much leaf and become small and forked if fresh manure is applied. On very poor soils use well-rotted compost; otherwise grow them after a crop for which the soil was manured the previous year.

Peas, runner beans and broad beans need organic matter to keep their roots moist. They can 'manufacture' their own nitrogen so rough compost, kitchen waste or even straw can be buried in a trench underneath them with no detrimental effects.

It is important that the individual needs of various crops, which may be quite different, are satisfied if they are to grow well. How this can be achieved when planning a vegetable plot is described on page 43.

Choosing varieties

Few gardens can produce enough for a household to be completely self-sufficient in vegetables. The selection of crops must depend first on the growing conditions in the garden, and then on space, time and personal preferences.

Vegetables such as carrots, cabbage, onions and potatoes can be worth growing at home, simply because they will taste better than those in the shops and will not be treated with chemicals. However, as organically grown vegetables become more widely available it may be practical to buy those that can be stored: this will make extra space available for ones that benefit from being freshly picked.

First among these are a whole range of salad crops – not just summer lettuces and radishes but the less common, hardy winter salads like landcress, lamb's lettuce, claytonia, cutting chicories and Chinese mustards. A garnish of green leaves from these plants will bring to life any winter salad or cooked dish, even if it is made from stored or frozen vegetables. Other vegetables best picked fresh are leafy crops such as spinach and kale, which go limp after a few hours, and peas and beans, which soon lose much of their sweetness.

You might also want to make space in the garden for unusual vegetables that are difficult or expensive to buy. Salsify, scorzonera, celeriac, Hamburg parsley and kohl rabi all come into this category, as do the unusual varieties of ordinary vegetables: yellow courgettes, golden beetroot and purple beans.

Some crops obviously need more attention than others, but the total time you can spend in the garden is not as important as how often and when. There are a few crops, such as potatoes and Jerusalem artichokes, that are easy to establish and need little regular care. Others, such as broad beans and courgettes, are robust once they are growing, but the crop must be picked frequently. Protection from pests can take up a lot of time: sprouts, for example, often need protection against slugs, birds, cabbage root fly, caterpillars and aphids – and sometimes need staking as well. Onions suffer few such problems, but need regular hoeing and hand weeding.

For every crop there is a wide range of varieties available, both old and new. The new varieties will have been bred for commercial growers who need crops that can be harvested mechanically and that still look attractive after a journey to the shops. Nevertheless, they also often have advantages for the gardener (see below).

Some of the old favourites still have qualities

Vegetables growing in small blocks in raised or fixed beds (see pages 20 and 45). The permanent paths are covered with shredded bark which not only looks attractive but keep feet dry in wet weather

that are hard to match, yet there is a danger that they will be dropped from catalogues. This is a fate that has already befallen many varieties because seedsmen have not considered them financially viable.

General points to look out for when choosing varieties from catalogues are:

- Sowing and harvesting times. These are important in planning a continuous supply. For example, carrot varieties described as 'early' are ready much quicker than 'main crop' varieties, but they will not store.

- F_1 hybrid varieties. The seed of these new varieties is expensive, but usually more reliable than that of traditional varieties. It produces crops that are more uniform. This can in fact be a disadvantage if it means that the whole crop is ready for harvesting at once – as with peas, for example. However, with crops like Brussels sprouts, where it reduces the number of poor quality plants, it is a distinct advantage.

- Yield and flavour. New varieties are often more productive, but this can be less important to the gardener than other factors, particularly taste, which is rarely mentioned in catalogue descriptions! However, both yield and flavour can depend as much on the way the crops are grown as on variety – over-generous watering of tomatoes, for example, tends to give large fruits without much taste.

- Disease and pest resistance. Now that chemical pesticides and fungicides are becoming expensive for commercial growers, more research is being carried out to breed varieties resistant to pests and diseases. This is a property of some new varieties that is well worth looking out for (see pages 54 and 55).

Experience is the best guide for deciding which crops you can grow successfully and which varieties you like best; there are some suggestions at the end of this chapter. Keeping a garden diary of sowing and planting dates and how each crop performed can be a great help.

Planning the layout of the vegetable garden

Rotation

A few perennial vegetables need permanent positions in the garden – asparagus, globe artichokes and seakale, for example. The rest should be rotated so that crops in the same botanical families or groups are not grown in the same ground year after year (see table on page 44). There are several reasons for this:

- It prevents pests and diseases building up in the soil. These are often specific to a particular family group: clubroot affects all brassicas, for example, and white rot affects onions, leeks and shallots. (More examples are given in the pests and disease charts, pages 53 to 55, and in the A to Z section.)

Cardoons are handsome vegetables and their stalks are blanched before cooking. Their flavour is reminiscent of globe artichokes

- It makes preparation of the soil with manures, fertilizers and lime more convenient, as crops liking the same treatment are kept together. It also means that a green manure can be grown on every part of the plot at some time.

- It makes a balanced use of the nutrients in the soil. Some crops are particularly 'hungry' for one element (e.g. tomatoes for potassium), and if they are grown continuously in one place they quickly deplete it. On the other hand, peas and beans add nitrogen to the soil, which can then be used by another crop.

- The different growth of the various crops helps the soil structure: deep-rooted crops like parsnips and spinach beet alternating with shallow, fibrous-rooted ones like lettuce, for example.

If your vegetable plot is large enough, think of it as divided into three or four different areas and plan a three- or four-year rotation of crops. A suggested plan is outlined below. Vegetables not included in the various rotation groups can fill in any gaps. In a small garden, or where there are other reasons for mixing the crops, simply try to avoid growing the same crop on the same piece of ground for two consecutive years.

Sowing and harvesting times

The sowing or planting times and the harvesting times should also be considered when planning where crops are to grow. If those that are harvested at about the same time are grown together, these patches can be cleared and made ready for subsequent crops or green manures. This need not interfere with the rotation. For example leeks, winter salads and spinach beet, which all overwinter, can be grown near each other, and similarly all the overwintering brassicas such as kale, Brussels sprouts and sprouting broccoli. If half-hardy crops such as tomatoes, sweetcorn and courgettes, which are all planted out at the same time, are grown on the same patch, it can be cleared in time for an overwintering green manure to be sown.

GROUPS OF VEGETABLES FOR PLANNING A ROTATION

Cabbage family (*Brassicas*)	Peas and bean family (*Legumes*)
BRUSSELS SPROUTS BROCCOLI CABBAGE (all kinds) CALABRESE CAULIFLOWER CHINESE MUSTARDS KALE KOHL RABI SWEDES TURNIPS	BROAD BEANS FRENCH BEANS RUNNER BEANS PEAS
	Potatoes (*Solanaceae*) POTATOES TOMATOES
Onion family (*Alliums*) GARLIC LEEKS ONIONS (all kinds) SHALLOTS	**Roots** (*Umbelliferae*) CARROTS CELERIAC HAMBURG PARSLEY PARSNIPS (*Chenopodiaceae*) BEETROOT (*Compositae*) SALSIFY SCORZONERA

A POSSIBLE FOUR-YEAR ROTATION

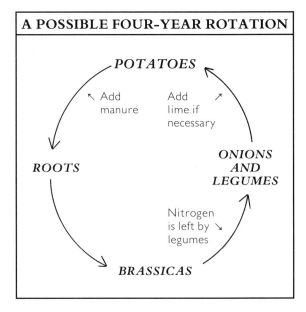

POTATOES

Add manure — Add lime if necessary

ROOTS

ONIONS AND LEGUMES

Nitrogen is left by legumes

BRASSICAS

Growing in raised or fixed beds

One convenient way of laying out a vegetable plot is in narrow beds separated by permanent paths, as described in Chapter 1. One of the main advantages is being able to work when it is wet without damaging the soil structure. Having a number of distinct beds also makes it easy to plan a workable rotation of crops. These are planted intensively, covering the whole surface of the bed, so weeds hardly get a chance to grow.

Vegetables in the flower border

Vegetables can look surprisingly attractive growing among ornamental plants. However, not all are suitable, and there are problems to be overcome:

- The soil needs to be more fertile for vegetables than it does for most flowers: overcome this by forking in compost locally and mulching.

- It is difficult for seedlings or small plants to compete with established perennials. Allow plenty of space for sowing and planting or stick to perennial vegetables like globe artichokes and asparagus.

- Gaps left on harvesting must not be too noticeable: continuous cropping plants such as chard, courgettes and climbing beans are best.

Crop spacing

Few gardening books agree on how vegetables should be spaced, and indeed there are no fixed rules. It is better to understand the consequences of changing the spacing and make your own judgements.

The spacing affects the size of the plants, the total yield and how easy – or difficult – it is to control weeds. As we have seen, an evenly distributed pattern is best for raised or fixed beds. On a conventional plot this makes hoeing and weeding more difficult but it may still be practical for some crops; for others, a compromise between this and the traditional system of closely spaced

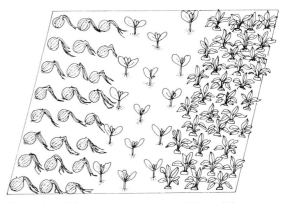

Crops should be planted in blocks with equidistant spacing rather than in rows. They can be planted closer together than on conventional plots because there is no need to walk between them and because the fertility of the beds is high. This usually compensates in yield for the growing area lost to pathways

ORNAMENTAL VEGETABLES	
ASPARAGUS SEAKALE	Perennial – foliage attractive when harvesting is over.
GLOBE ARTICHOKES	Perennial – silver-grey leaves and handsome flowerheads; only one or two cut from each plant at any one time.
CLIMBING FRENCH BEANS RUNNER BEANS	Attractive flowers, pods picked over a long period.
COURGETTES (green and yellow) SQUASHES AND CUCUMBERS	Attractive flowers, foliage unaffected by picking. Squashes and cucumbers can climb up a trellis or wigwam of canes.
CUTTING LETTUCE SWISS CHARD RUBY CHARD RED-LEAVED CHICORY	Attractive leaves – just a few from each plant picked at a time.
SALSIFY	Some roots left to produce edible shoots and attractive flowers in their second year.

A conventional crop planting in rows makes weeding and hoeing easier, but traditional spacings are not necessarily the best

lettuce, turnips or even small summer cabbages can be cropped between Brussels sprouts, and radishes between parsnips.

This 'intercropping' is not always as easy as it sounds. It must be timed so that the quick crop is harvested before it interferes with the main crop or gets swamped out itself. Nevertheless, it can give useful extra yields from a small space.

Sometimes low-growing or trailing crops can have more permanent positions between tall ones without either of them suffering. For example, New Zealand spinach or cucumbers can be left to spread among sweetcorn.

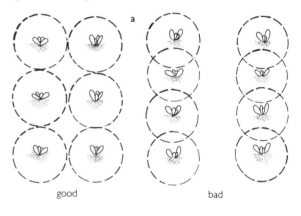

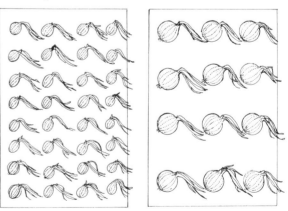

(a) The circles represent the area from which the plants take water and nutrients from the soil. The evenly spaced crop makes better use of these resources
(b) Onions planted close together will be smaller, but both the number and the total weight will be higher

plants in widely spaced rows may be more appropriate.

In either case, the closer the plants the more they compete with one another and the smaller they end up. However, this can be an advantage: many people would prefer a lot of small onions, for example, to a few large ones, and the total yield – that is, the total weight of onion – can be greater. Of course there comes a point where closing up the spacing still further produces plants that are too small, and the overall yield begins to decrease. Some suggested spacings for the various crops are shown in the illustration.

When there are large spaces between plants that are slow to mature, a quick-growing crop can sometimes be sown or planted. For example,

Vegetables all the year round

It is possible to eat homegrown organic vegetables all the year round, even from a small garden. The first welcome fresh supplies come from protected early sowings, and similar protection can extend the season of tender crops well into the autumn. In summer, careful planning can give a continuous supply of produce and plenty of choice – it is a good time to try some of the more unusual crops. For winter, many root crops can be lifted and stored; these can be supplemented by leafy brassicas and winter salads left in the ground.

Early crops

The calendar is an unreliable guide for early sowings, as the 'coming of spring' can vary by a month or more. In the garden you can relate it to the growth of the grass, the flowering of the spring bulbs and shrubs and even the appearance of certain weeds. As explained in Chapter 1, the critical factor for seed sowing is the soil temperature. The minimum temperatures needed for the

germination of certain vegetable seeds are given in the table below. This gives an idea of the order of sowings, even if you do not have a soil thermometer. The earliest crops to be sown and harvested are radishes, spring turnips, lettuce, early peas and broad beans.

Sowings can be made earlier and are more reliable if they are protected by cloches – these raise the soil temperature and also keep off heavy rain and birds. Glass cloches keep in the most heat and let in most light, but the modern plastic ones also work well. In fact the soil temperature can be usefully raised simply by covering the seedbed with a clear plastic sheet for about a week before sowing, and afterwards replacing it until the seeds just begin to germinate.

A useful extension of this idea is the 'floating'

'Floating' cloche or mulch can be cut to any size and will protect germinating seeds and young plants

TEMPERATURE RANGE FOR SUCCESSFUL GERMINATION	
LETTUCE (except 'crisp' varieties)	0°–25°C (32°–77°F)
LETTUCE ('crisp' varieties)	0°–29°C (22°–84°F)
BRASSICAS, PEAS, BROAD BEANS	5°–32°C (41°–90°F)
LEEKS AND ONIONS	7°–24°C (45°–75°F)
CARROTS, PARSNIPS, BEETROOT	over 7°C (45°F)
CELERY	10°–19°C (50°–66°F)
CUCUMBERS, MARROW, COURGETTES, PUMPKINS	over 13°C (56°F)
FRENCH AND RUNNER BEANS TOMATOES, SWEETCORN	over 12°C (55°F)

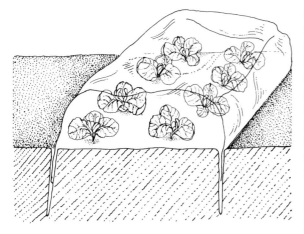

Protective 'floating' film should be spread loosely over the crop and then secured in slits about 5 cm (2 in) deep on either side

cloche or mulch. This is a very light perforated or woven plastic film which can be laid over newly sown or planted crops and will to some extent expand as they grow. Some vegetables, such as radish, can be left covered until harvest, but others need to be exposed before the film begins to cause restriction.

Sowing seeds indoors and transplanting them is another way to hasten the start of the vegetable season. This is essential for tender crops like tomatoes and cucumbers, and for slow growers like celery and celeriac, which would otherwise not mature before the end of summer. It is also useful for lettuce and summer cabbage to get much earlier crops. To minimize the shock of transplanting, sowings are best made in individual pots or divided trays (see Chapter 1). Some crops are not suited to transplanting, for example all root crops – carrots, beetroot, turnips and swedes.

Successional sowings

Some crops need only one sowing, because they either stay in the ground in good condition (like parsnips) or produce a succession of leaves or fruit from the one plant (like spinach beet or courgettes). Others must be sown at intervals in order to produce a continuous supply – lettuce, radish, peas, French beans and spring onions, for example. It is thus important to know roughly how long they take to mature. This may depend on variety (see page 41), but at the height of the growing season you would perhaps expect to sow radish every two weeks, lettuce every three and spring onions every four. In general, the higher the temperature the faster they grow, so that sowing intervals in spring and late summer will need to be longer than those in mid summer.

Very high soil temperatures can, however, prevent the germination of some seeds – most notably lettuce (see page 47); watering the seed bed and sowing late in the evening during a heatwave will help to overcome this problem.

Many leafy salads will grow again after being cut at an early stage, and this 'cut and come again' technique can be used to produce crops quickly and to save resowing. Suitable crops include salad rape and mustard, claytonia, corn salad, Chinese mustards and cutting types of lettuce and chicory. The seed can be broadcast or sown in close rows. The leaves can be cut when the crop is only about 5–7.5 cm (2–3 in) high, and then again in two to four weeks, depending on the time of year and the temperature.

Winter crops

Late summer is the time for sowing winter salads: landcress, lamb's lettuce, claytonia, red chicory and some of the Chinese mustards. Many of these can be cut throughout a mild winter and begin growing very early in spring – a preferable alternative to the insipid greenhouse lettuce offered by the greengrocer. Leaf beet and Swiss chard will also grow from late summer sowings and will generally overwinter, especially if given some protection in severe weather.

The most familiar crops in the ground over winter come from spring sowings of leeks, cabbages, sprouts, broccoli and kale – and roots like parsnip, salsify and Jerusalem artichokes. These can be supplemented by stored supplies of potatoes, onions and other root crops.

Vegetable storage

Vegetables can be stored successfully only if they are of good quality and are harvested carefully at the right time. Organically grown vegetables are said to keep particularly well. This could be because they often contain less water than conventionally grown crops and have a healthy resistance to storage rots. However, they must be given the correct conditions, both of temperature and of humidity.

Onions should be lifted when their leaves have fallen over – certainly by mid September – and laid out in a warm, airy place until they are completely dry. They can then be laced into the traditional ropes or put in nets and hung in a cold, dry place where there is good ventilation. There is little danger that they will suffer frost damage or dry out.

Potatoes should be dug up in late autumn, while conditions are still not too wet, and left on the surface for a few hours to dry off. In store they need to have some air and to be kept well above freezing – ideally above 4°c (39°F). They are usually put in double thickness paper sacks and

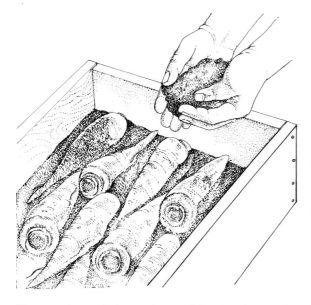

Store root crops between layers of damp peat or sand in wooden boxes, and keep them in cold places

stored in an outbuilding, but they must be given extra protection with blankets and carpet in severe weather. Pumpkins and marrows brought in before the first frosts need similar conditions.

Root crops, on the other hand, need to be kept moist to prevent them drying out. They store very successfully if laid in wooden boxes or plastic bins between layers of damp sand or peat, but it is sufficient to seal them in polythene bags in small quantities. They must be kept cold – only just above freezing, if possible. This treatment is ideal for carrots, turnips, beetroot and celeriac, which should be lifted in late autumn before the most severe weather.

Weed control and watering

Judiciously timed weeding and watering all help towards getting a good yield from crops that are not boosted by artificial fertilizers. In an established organic garden neither should present much of a problem.

Weeding

Once the ground is clear of most perennial weeds (see Chapter 1), annuals among vegetable crops can be dealt with by hoeing, hand weeding and mulching. Ideally there should be little space for weeds to grow!

It is most important to prevent competition from weeds when plants are young. Once the crop is established, the canopy formed by their leaves will prevent weed seeds from germinating nearby – and when vegetables like beetroot are grown at an equidistant spacing, their broad leaves often close up the gaps so that only the occasional weed will penetrate.

More hoeing will be needed between narrow-leaved crops such as leeks and onions, and here a mulch of dry lawn mowings, leafmould or well-rotted compost can help suppress weeds. Coarser mulches such as old hay can be used where there is

A mulch of dry lawn mowings or old hay spread thickly around courgettes retains moisture and prevents competition from weeds

space between crop rows to allow for picking, and strawy manure is suitable between widely spaced crops like courgettes and brassicas. Similar mulches can be used on temporary vacant patches, though if there is time for a green manure to be sown, this will also prevent weeds growing.

Finally, remember that all weeds are not bad all the time (see Chapter 1). Where there is no competition with the crop they can sometimes be a help – for example, in protecting a mature root crop from frost.

Watering

Transplanted plants should be watered until they become established, but after this regular watering is not always necessary or even desirable. Over-watering can damage the soil structure. It also encourages leafy plants to make only shallow roots, and root crops to make excess leaf growth, and it can adversely affect the flavour of all crops.

A well-structured organic soil retains moisture and allows plant roots to spread widely to extract what they need – and no more. This is one reason why organically grown vegetables have such a good flavour. Mulching (as for weed control) will also play an important part in preventing water loss from the soil, especially between widely spaced crops.

However, there are times during the life of a crop when watering can be beneficial. Leafy crops respond at any stage by an increase in 'edible' growth. Peas, beans, tomatoes and cucumbers benefit most when they start to flower and to produce pods, and potatoes just after the tubers are formed (this approximately coincides with flowering). Root vegetables should need little watering but the soil should not be allowed to get very dry, or splitting may occur when it rains.

Whatever and whenever you are watering, always water well, soaking the soil to a depth of several inches. One of the most efficient ways to water is with a length of 'trickle' or 'seep' hose – a flat hose with small holes in it which is laid on the ground between plants. This can be put beneath a mulch that would prevent moisture penetrating from above.

Pest and disease control

Vegetables benefit from all the advantages of an organically managed garden mentioned in Chapter 1. If the soil is well cared for, the plants will be healthy and able to stand up to most pests and diseases. Encourage diversity by planting flowers and shrubs as well as fruit and vegetables, then no one pest or disease is likely to build up to a harmful level. Provide additional help by growing flowers that attract the natural enemies of insect pests.

There are also a few methods of avoiding attacks that are particularly applicable to vegetables. The detail relating to the different crops (see pages 56–65) can be complicated, but the general principles are easy to understand. Because most vegetable crops are annuals and are cleared after harvest, it should be possible to break the cycle of infection from one crop to the next. An obvious example is the rotation of crops within the garden (see page 43); moving each family group to a different spot each year will help to prevent the build-up of soil pests and diseases.

Garden hygiene

With pests and fungi that spread above the ground, it is important to remove and compost or burn all infected plant debris. Carrot fly larvae, for example, can overwinter in old carrots left in the ground, and downy mildew fungi remain on discarded cabbage leaves. Some of the greatest threats are to brassicas, as overwintered plants are often still in the ground when the first spring ones are planted. Old Brussels sprout and cabbage stalks left after the crop has been picked can harbour mealy aphids and cabbage root fly larvae, and should be dug up as soon as possible.

Some weeds can host particular pests and diseases during the times that there are no crops. Chickweed, for example, can carry a virus – cucumber mosaic virus – that attacks lettuces, marrows and cucumbers. It should therefore be composted or dug in if the disease has been a problem during the growing season.

When vegetables are cleared, digging or forking over the bed will expose some soil pests to the weather and to the birds. This is certainly worth doing on patches where cutworms, wireworms or leatherjackets have been a problem, though it may mean that this area has to miss out on an over-wintering green manure.

Sowing and planting dates

The times of sowing or planting a crop can sometimes be planned to avoid the worst periods of attack by particular pests. For example, autumn or early spring sowings of broad beans should be almost fully grown by the time the black bean aphids arrive. Similarly, peas sown early or very late miss much of the damage caused by the pea moth larvae – the unwelcome maggots found inside the pods in high summer. Where there is more than one generation of a pest in the year, as is

the case with carrot fly, the seasonable weather has an increasingly important effect, and timing the sowing becomes more difficult. However, it can become almost intuitive after a while and can help considerably towards getting a trouble-free crop.

Resistant varieties

Many new varieties of vegetables have been selected for their resistance to certain pests and diseases. There are lettuces resistant to root aphid and downy mildew, and some potatoes are less susceptible to blight than others. More examples are given in the A to Z section.

Barriers and traps

Understanding the life cycle of vegetable pests has in several cases led to specific and very successful methods of avoiding damage. For example, when a young cabbage or sprout plant does not grow away like its neighbours, it usually means that the roots are being eaten by the small white grubs that are the larvae of the cabbage root fly. The adult fly lays its eggs where the stem of a brassica plant meets the soil and the hatching larvae burrow down to feed. The flies can be prevented from laying by placing a small mat, cut from carpet

Mats of a spongy material protect brassica plants against cabbage root fly. They should be cut to about 12.5 cm (5 in) in diameter or square. Make a small central hole in each and slit to the edge so that it can be slipped easily round the young plant

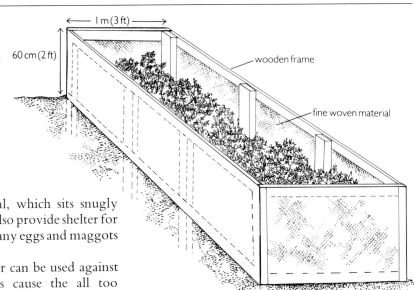

A barrier set up round rows of carrots before or just after sowing. The frame can be made of wood or posts and wire. Wood makes it easy to attach the barrier material, which can be of clear polythene – or preferably of a finely meshed windbreak/shading material, which stands up better in the wind

underlay or similar material, which sits snugly round each plant. The mats also provide shelter for beneficial beetles, which eat any eggs and maggots that are present.

A different type of barrier can be used against carrot fly, whose maggots cause the all too familiar labyrinth of tunnels in carrot roots. In this case a barrier is put up round the whole carrot bed. It seems that the carrot fly skims in low onto the crops, and the barrier effectively prevents them from landing.

Other methods of avoiding damage rely on disguising the scent of the carrots, which attracts the pest from a considerable distance. Sow the seed sparsely so there is no need to thin the seedlings (crushed foliage gives off more scent). Interplanting the rows of carrots with onions has been shown to work – but the effect is only significant if there are many more onions than carrots. However, any interplanting or mulching can only help.

The cabbage root fly identifies brassica plants by sight as well as by smell, and young plants silhouetted against bare earth are easy to recognize. Thus it can be advantageous to interplant widely spaced brassicas with a different, quick-maturing crop, or to alternate the rows of brassicas with another main crop. The closely woven 'floating mulches' made for frost protection (see pages 47 and 48) can equally well be used to protect young brassica plants and seedlings from cabbage root fly, caterpillars and fleabeetle.

Slugs cause some of the worst damage to young vegetable plants and there is no easy organic answer. They can be trapped in various ways – saucers of beer sunk into the ground and half grapefruit skins are often recommended. If you empty and replenish traps regularly, such devices can significantly reduce the number of slugs in the garden, but they will not entice those that are left away from a row of newly transplanted lettuces. However, small numbers of plants can be protected effectively with barriers made from plastic lemonade bottles; these are removed as the plants grow larger. Similar, narrower collars pressed well into the ground will act as a barrier against cutworms and can be left on to protect the stems of susceptible plants such as courgettes.

Are perfect crops necessary?

No one wants to grow or eat vegetables that are infested with bugs or spoilt by disease, but not all damage is necessarily harmful. For example, the holes that fleabeetles make in mature turnip or radish leaves affect neither the look of the edible part of the crop nor its yield. Even some blemishes on the crop itself can be acceptable: a few holes in the outer leaves of cabbages are a small inconvenience compared to the harm that slug pellets do.

With a little tolerance and care, it is possible to live happily with most garden insects and grow productive and appetising crops too.

PESTS AFFECTING LEAVES AND FRUIT OF VEGETABLE CROPS

Pests	Crops affected	Description/symptoms	Control
BIRDS	Brassica plants, peas and young seedlings are most affected.	Pigeons are often the worst culprits for devastating brassicas, particularly young plants and overwintering greens. Sparrows and other garden birds go for seedlings, with lettuce and spinach among their favourites.	Floating mulches will protect seedlings (see pages 47 and 48) and netting is worthwhile for a small area. Scarers like milkbottle tops on string or coloured strips of polythene flapping in the wind can work for a time, but change them around – birds can get used to almost anything!
BLACK BEAN APHID (Blackfly)	Commonest on broad beans, but also attacks French and runner beans	Groups of blackfly first appear on the tip of the plant about late May and spread downwards onto pods and leaves.	Pinch out tips containing colonies provided that the plants have grown enough to give a good crop – about five flower trusses should have formed (getting a good start with autumn sown beans or using cloches helps). Spray with insectidal soap or derris (see page 36).
CABBAGE APHID	Brassicas	Grey-green mealy aphid.	Small colonies on mature leaves can be squashed. Spray with insectidal soap or derris. Remove old leaves and stems left in the soil after harvest.
CABBAGE WHITEFLY	Brassicas	Tiny pure white flies rise in swarms when affected plants are touched.	
CATERPILLARS	Most brassicas	Green or black and yellow caterpillars eat holes in leaves.	Inspect plants regularly and pick off and destroy caterpillars before they multiply or spray with *Bacillus thuringiensis* (see page 36).
CELERY FLY	Celery, celeriac, parsnip	Brown blisters on leaves formed by tiny tunnelling larvae.	Reject any seedlings with blistered leaves; pinch off and burn any infected leaves on bigger plants as soon as symptoms appear. Spray with nicotine and soft soap in very severe attacks.
FLEABEETLE	All brassicas, particularly young plants	Small (3 mm/$\frac{1}{8}$ in) shiny beetles eat many circular holes in leaves; they jump away when plants are touched.	Keep young seedlings growing quickly by weeding and watering; dust rows with derris and give a tonic of liquid seaweed where necessary. Alternatively, protect them with a floating mulch. Damage on the leaves of mature plants, especially radish, swedes and turnips, does not affect the crop significantly. Radish, swede and turnip sown in June often miss the worst attacks. The beetles overwinter in patches of weeds and debris.
LETTUCE APHIDS	Lettuce – especially in dry conditions	Colonies of greenish aphids on undersides of leaves and in heart.	Spray with insectidal soap or derris.
PEA AND BEAN WEEVIL	Peas and broad beans	'Bites' taken from edges of leaves.	Keep seedlings growing strongly, start broad beans inside and early peas under cloches, dust rows with derris. Mature plants should not be harmed. The weevils overwinter in weeds and debris.
PEA MOTH	Peas	Small white caterpillars in the pods.	February sowings that mature in June should miss the worst attacks, as should June sowings. Pupates in the soil over winter, so cultivation helps.
SLUGS	Most young plants, particularly lettuce and brassicas. Worst in wet conditions.	Young shoots eaten off. Holes in leaves.	Provide 'lemonade bottle' barriers round individual plants where practical (see page 32). Reduce slug numbers by handpicking and trapping. Keep area round young plants dry with a mulch of a material like coarse dry peat.

PESTS AFFECTING ROOTS AND BULBS OF VEGETABLE CROPS

Pests	Crops affected	Description/symptoms	Control
CABBAGE ROOT FLY	All brassicas	Young plants of cabbage, sprouts, etc. wilt and die; older plants remain stunted, and when they are dug up white maggots will be found on the roots. The surface of turnips, swedes and radish become mined with channels.	Dig up and destroy plants of cabbage, sprouts, etc. when symptoms appear, and dig up all plants immediately after harvest. Surround the base of each plant with a small mat of spongy material (see page 51). Interplant where possible (see page 52). Damage to large mature turnips and swedes is usually superficial.
CARROT FLY	Carrots, parsnips, celery, celeriac	Young seedlings die; foliage of older plants redden in a bad attack. Tunnels made by the fly larvae are found in the mature roots when they are lifted.	Avoid thinning; sow between row of onions or mulch the rows to mask the 'carrot' smell. Surround carrot bed with a plastic or fine mesh barrier (see page 52). Sow in March or early June to avoid attacks on seedlings.
CUTWORMS	Most crops, especially lettuce, courgettes, marrows, roots and potatoes	Greenish-grey caterpillars cut through stems at soil level and make holes in root crops and potatoes.	Place collars round individual plants and press them into the soil (see page 32). Heavy watering in June/July reduces damage. Cultivate soil in winter.
LEATHERJACKETS	Most crops, especially young lettuce and brassicas	Brown grubs bite through stems at soil level and make ragged holes in lower leaves.	Commonly found under pasture and in damp places, so expect trouble in ground just brought into cultivation; good drainage helps. Dig up the roots of cut off plants – the culprit may still be harbouring there. Cultivate soil in winter. Cutworm collars may help individual plants (see page 32).
LETTUCE ROOT APHID	Lettuce	Plants wilt and die. Colonies of white aphids are visible on roots when plants are lifted.	Destroy infected plants. Do not grow lettuce continuously in the same place. Use resistant varieties.
ONION FLY	Onions, leeks and shallots	Maggots attack seedlings, which die off in groups, and burrow into bulbs.	Avoid thinning sown crops. Sets and plants raised in a greenhouse are large enough to be less vulnerable at the time of the first attacks. Dig up and burn affected plants. Cultivate the soil in winter.
POTATO CYST EELWORM	Potatoes, tomatoes	Plants stunted, tubers and tomato fruits small. Tiny white or brown cysts visible on roots in mid summer.	Buy seed potatoes from a reliable source. Do not grow potatoes on infected land for at least six years. Try a resistant variety.
SLUGS	Potatoes and all root crops	Holes in roots and tubers	Cultivate soil in winter. Use least susceptible potato varieties.
STEM AND BULB EELWORM	Leeks, onions	Microscopic worm-like creatures which cause stunting of seedlings, and thickening and rotting of plants.	Remove and destroy infected plants, Practise a strict crop rotation, so that leeks and onions are not grown on the same land for at least three years.
WIREWORMS (Click beetle larvae)	Many, especially potato and root crops	Thin orange 'worms' eat holes in roots and tubers and nip off stems below soil level.	Most common in neglected ground and pasture land, feeding on roots just below the surface, so they cause most trouble in ground just brought into cultivation. Avoid roots and potatoes for about three years where such problems occur (it takes this long for the larvae to become beetles and fly away). Cultivate the soil in winter.

DISEASES AFFECTING VEGETABLE CROPS

Pests	Crops affected	Description/symptoms	Control
CANKER	Parsnips	Roots become brown and cracked and eventually rot.	Rotate crops and lime acid soils; use resistant varieties. May sowings are often less affected.
CLUBROOT	All brassicas	Discoloured leaves; wilting plants; swollen roots.	Keep soil well drained; lime if necessary so it is slightly alkaline. Rotate all brassica crops. Once soil becomes infected disease will last for up to 20 years. Dig up and burn infected plants. Use resistant varieties. Raise plants in potting compost to give them a good start.
DAMPING OFF	All seedlings	Seedlings do not emerge, or wither soon afterwards.	Avoid sowing in cold, wet soils; sow thinly.
DOWNY MILDEW	Brassicas, lettuce, onions and peas	Yellowing leaves with white spores underneath. Worse in cold, wet weather.	Remove diseased leaves or plants. Avoid overcrowding.
GREY MOULD (*Botrytis*)	Many, particularly French beans, lettuce and tomatoes	Grey mould on leaves and fruit; worse in wet weather.	Remove diseased parts of plant. Avoid overcrowding.
LEAF SPOTS	Broad beans, beetroot, spinach beet, brassicas, celery	Caused by a number of fungi. Usually seen as brown spots on leaves and sometimes stems.	Plants short of potash are sometimes more susceptible. Fork in a sprinkling of seaweed meal before sowing, and use rock potash for a long-term effect. Remove infected leaves at first signs of an attack. Do not overcrowd plants.
POTATO BLIGHT	Potatoes, tomatoes	Brown patches on leaves late in season; infected tubers rot in store.	Worse in warm, wet summers. Maincrop potatoes most affected; some varieties are partly resistant. Buy seed potatoes from a reliable source. If leaves become badly affected, cut off haulms and compost well or burn; wait about three weeks before digging tubers. Tomatoes under glass are less likely to be infected.
POWDERY MILDEW	Peas and beans, brassicas, cucumbers and marrows	White powdery mould on leaves and stems.	Worse in hot, dry conditions. Avoid overcrowding. Build up light soils with organic matter. Water and mulch plants.
ROOT AND FOOT ROTS	All roots (especially carrots), peas and beans	Caused by a number of fungi – usually specific to one crop. Various symptoms: dark brown, sunken patches on carrots; stems of beans blacken at the base.	Destroy infected plants. Avoid sowing in heavy, wet soil. Rotate crops.
SCAB	Potatoes	Scabby area on tubers. Does not affect inside of tuber or yield.	Worse on light, limy soils. Dig in organic matter and put grass mowings in trench to increase acidity. Use resistant varieties.
VIRUS DISEASES	Many crops	Various symptoms include mottling and distortion of leaves and fruit; sometimes stunting of whole plant.	Remove and burn infected plants. Buy seed from a reputable source. Grow resistant varieties where available, e.g. lettuce resistant to mosaic virus. Remove weeds which harbour disease, e.g. groundsel and shepherd's purse carry a lettuce virus, and chickweed carries cucumber mosaic virus. Control aphids which spread the disease.
WHITE ROT	Onions, leeks	Yellow, wilting foliage; white mould at base; stunted plants	Destroy infected plants. Rotate crops – disease persists for many years in soil.

Artichokes, globe

Handsome, silver-leaved, perennial plants, grown for fleshy flowerheads. A luxury crop, growing up to 90 cm (3 ft) high and taking up a great deal of space, but attractive enough for flowerbeds.

CONDITIONS Sunny, well-drained, fertile site; dig in plenty of well-rotted manure and a handful of hoof and horn per plant.

GROWING Can be grown from seed sown in pots in spring or from offsets from established plants (these are more reliably hardy). Plant out 75–90 cm (2½–3 ft) apart. Mulch with hay and grass mowings or strawy manure. Give crowns protection over winter, especially in their first year.

Artichokes, Jerusalem

Knobbly tubers produced under plants that can reach more than 2 m (6 ft) high. A very hardy winter crop that can be grown as a screen or in places not suitable for other crops.

CONDITIONS Tolerant of partial shade and most soils that are reasonably fertile.

GROWING Plant tubers from February to April, 10–15 cm (4–6 in) deep, 30–38 cm (12–15 in) apart. Support stems in summer and pinch out tops to restrict height to 2 m (6 ft). Dig tubers as required during the winter, and remove all tubers by spring or they can become invasive.

Beans, broad

Most varieties grow to 90 cm (3 ft) or more, but there are dwarf ones only 38 cm (15 in) tall. Hardy, one of the first summer crops. Roots fix nitrogen in the soil.

CONDITIONS Open site; reasonably fertile soil, preferably manured the previous winter, well drained for autumn sowing.

GROWING In mild districts some varieties can be sown in November to overwinter, but these are often attacked by soil pests and mice; those sown in early spring in pots indoors can crop almost as early. Plant out 23 cm (9 in) apart in rows 38 cm (15 in) apart or 30 cm (1 ft) apart each way. Later sowings can be made up until May, but these are often badly affected by blackfly (see page 53).

Beans, French

Most types are dwarf (about 45 cm, 1½ ft) but some climb – useful if slugs are a problem. Pods can be round or flat; purple, green, or yellow and waxy (these last are the most tender). Not very hardy.

CONDITIONS Open, sheltered site; light, moisture-retentive soil, well manured the previous winter.

GROWING Sow in trays or pots in April or outdoors May to July, 5–7.5 cm (2–3 in) deep, never in cold, wet conditions. Space plants 15 cm (6 in) apart each way.

Beans, runner

Most types climb, up to 3.7 m (12 ft); there are dwarf types but these do not produce such long, straight beans. Climbers have red, pink or white flowers and can look very attractive. Roots fix nitrogen in the soil. Not hardy.

CONDITIONS Warm, sheltered site; deep, rich, moisture-retentive soil – bury organic matter in a trench beneath row (see page 18).

GROWING Sow in trays or pots in early May, or mid–end May outside. Space plants 15 cm (6 in) apart in double rows 60 cm (2 ft) apart, or 30 cm (1 ft) apart in wigwams. Support with canes, string or netting. Mulch and water if dry.

Beetroot

Roots can be round or cylindrical; yellow or white, as well as the familiar purple. Use for summer salads or winter storage; young leaves can be cooked like spinach.

CONDITIONS Open site; light soil, not freshly manured but composted for the previous crop. Use calcified seaweed to provide lime and minerals on poor soils.

GROWING For early crops sow bolt-resistant varieties like 'Avonearly' in situ late March, in rows 20 cm (8 in) apart, and thin seedlings to 2.5 cm (1 in), or space 5 cm (2 in) apart each way. For later use and storage, sow May/June in rows 20 cm (8 in) apart and thin to 7.5 cm (3 in), or space 10 cm (4 in) apart each way.

Broccoli, purple sprouting

Large, spreading plants up to 90 cm (3 ft) tall, but they justify the space as they can be picked in early spring when little else is available. Hardy.

CONDITIONS Sheltered, well-drained site; rich soil; well composted or manured, and limed if acid.

GROWING Sow April-mid May in a seed bed, soil blocks or trays, and plant out in June to mid July 60 cm

(2 ft) each way. Earth up stems, water, mulch during the summer, and stake in exposed areas.

Brussels sprouts

Plants grow 45–105 cm ($1\frac{1}{2}$–$3\frac{1}{2}$ ft) high depending on variety. F_1 hybrids are more reliable and worth buying. Look for disease-resistant varieties, e.g. 'Rampart', resistant to downy mildew. Hardy.

CONDITIONS Open site; rich, moisture-retentive soil, manured the previous winter; lime if acid.

GROWING Sow mid March to mid April in a seed bed, soil blocks or trays; plant out May/June 75–90 cm (2–3 ft) apart each way. Earth up stems, water and mulch; stake if necessary. Remove yellow leaves to prevent fungal diseases. Dress with fish, blood and bone or seaweed meal in mid summer on poor soils.

Cabbages

Different types can be used to provide cabbages all the year round for salads and cooking. Compact varieties like 'Hispi' (F_1) are best for intensive planting. Some varieties, especially the Savoys, are very hardy.

CONDITIONS Open site; rich, moisture-retentive soil; composted or manured, and limed if acid.

GROWING Sow in a seed bed, trays or soil blocks and plant out firmly.

Spring cabbage: Sow early August, plant out mid September to mid October, 30 cm (12 in) apart each way. Dress with blood, fish and bone or seaweed meal in early spring.

Summer cabbage: Sow February/March indoors, March to May outdoors; plant out May to July, 30–45 cm (12–18in) each way.

Winter cabbage (includes red and white salad cabbages): Sow April/May; plant out mid to end July.

Calabrese

Produces green, broccoli-like side shoots for several months in mid summer/early autumn after the main head has been cut. Not very hardy.

CONDITIONS As for cabbages.

GROWING Sow April/May *in situ* or in divided trays or soil blocks (*not* a seed bed). Plant out in June, 30 cm (12 in) apart each way.

Carrots

Short, quick-maturing types ('Amsterdam' and 'Nantes' varieties) for small summer carrots; larger, slow-growing types (like 'Autumn King' and 'Berlicum' varieties) for winter use.

CONDITIONS Light but fertile soil, *not* freshly manured or stony.

GROWING Sow March to June for summer crops, late May for winter use. Sow sparingly in drills 15 cm (6 in) apart and thin maincrop varieties to 5 cm (2 in) apart (earlies should not need thinning). On fixed beds sow in bands, thinning early carrots to 5 cm (2 in) apart each way and maincrop to 10 cm (4 in). Hand weeding is important in early stages; later mulch with lawn mowings, which may also help to deter carrot flies. If this pest is a problem, arrange sowings so that a barrier can be erected (see page 52).

Cauliflower

Varieties can be chosen to crop at different times – from early spring to late autumn in mild districts – but many take up a lot of space for a long time and may fail if there is any check to growth. Early summer varieties are best value; on fixed beds sow intensively to produce mini-cauliflowers with 5–7.5 cm (2–3 in) heads.

CONDITIONS Rich, moisture-retentive soil, but not freshly manured, and avoid any fertilizer high in nitrogen.

GROWING **Early summer varieties**: Sow in pots early October, overwinter in cold greenhouse, plant out mid March, 53 cm (21 in) each way. For mini-cauliflowers, sow *in situ* April to June, spacing 15 cm (6 in) each way, cut July to October.

Late summer varieties: Sow in April in soil blocks, trays or seed bed and plant out 53 cm (21 in) each way.

Autumn varieties: Sow in blocks or seed bed in mid May, plant out 60 cm (2 ft) each way. To minimize growth checks, always transplant as soon as plants are ready and conditions are right. Mulch and keep well watered during dry spells.

Celeriac

Grown for its swollen stem base, which can often replace celery in salads or cooking. Hardier and less prone to pests and diseases than celery, but lift and store before severe weather.

CONDITIONS Open site; rich, moisture-retentive soil, compost before planting.

GROWING Needs a long growing season: sow indoors in March, with heat if possible, in blocks or trays. Plant out in May, 30–38 cm (12–15 in) apart each way; mulch and keep watered in dry spells. Remove oldest leaves from the base of the bulb in late summer.

Celery (self-blanching)

Trench celery is fairly hardy but takes a lot of space and is difficult to grow well. Self-blanching types are better value but are not so hardy. Any check to growth leads to bolting.

CONDITIONS As for celeriac.

GROWING Sow, plant out and water as for celeriac 15–28cm (6–11in) apart each way.

Chicory (cutting)

There are several distinct types of chicory: the Whitloof type, whose roots are forced indoors in winter; the sugar loaf type, which forms dense heads but is not very hardy; and the hardy red and green cutting types, which sometimes form small heads but are most useful for a continuous supply of young leaves. This last type, which can be grown almost all the year round, includes the red Italian chicories and very hard 'grumolo' varieties; sugar loaf varieties can be mixed in for a summer seedling crop.

CONDITIONS Will grow on most soils, but a sheltered, well-drained site is best for winter crops; a weed-free seed bed is needed for broadcast seeds.

GROWING Sow red chicories May/June, broadcast in patches or spaced 13 cm (5 in) each way. Young green leaves can be cut in summer, red leaves appear in winter and early spring. Sow patches of sugar loaf (for a seedling crop) and grumolo types April to July.

Chinese cabbage

Most types form dense hearts in late summer to early autumn; cook or eat raw. Not very hardy but a useful quick-growing crop to sow after early crops are harvested. Will bolt if sown too early or growth checked. New F_1 varieties are the most reliable.

CONDITIONS Fairly sunny site; very rich, moisture-retentive soil, limed if acid.

GROWING Sow *in situ* June/July in rows 30 cm (12 in) apart, and thin plants to 30 cm (12 in). Use a floating mulch (see page 47) if fleabeetle is a problem. Keep very well watered.

Chinese mustards

Quick-growing crops – leaves, stalks and sometimes flowering shoots are used. Good for autumn/winter/early spring salads. Examples are 'Chinese Pak Choi' (not very hardy, leaves and stalks used), 'Mizuna'

Opposite: Cabbages and lettuces can look attractive enough to grow amongst ornamental plants in a small garden

'Mizuna' is one of the quick-growing Chinese mustard crops suitable for winter salads

(fairly hardy, leaves and stalks used; attractive in flower beds), 'Green-in-the-Snow' (very hardy, leaves used).

CONDITIONS As Chinese cabbage, but not quite so fussy.

GROWING Sow *in situ* late June to August; thin to 15–30 cm (6–12 in) apart depending on variety.

Courgettes

Any immature marrows can be used, but compact, high-yielding bush forms sold especially for courgettes are best and can be attractive – there are green, striped and yellow types.

CONDITIONS Sunny, sheltered site, fairly rich soil; a site can be prepared for each plant by filling a hole with about a bucketful of rotted manure or compost and covering with 15 cm (6 in) of soil.

GROWING Sow indoors in pots in gentle heat in mid April, plant out end May/early June when all risk of frost is past. Space 60 cm (2 ft) apart. Alternatively, sow two or three seeds *in situ* under jam jars in late May and thin out weakest seedlings to leave one plant. Mulch and water in dry spells. Feeding with comfrey liquids when plants start to fruit is beneficial. Pick fruit regularly.

Cucumbers (outdoor)

Traditional 'ridge' cucumbers are prickly and bulbous, but modern Japanese outdoor varieties look more like greenhouse cucumbers; they are also more tolerant of poor weather conditions. There is also an attractive, pale, round ridge cucumber, 'Crystal Apple'.

CONDITIONS AND GROWING As for courgettes, but space plants 90 cm (3 ft) apart if grown on the flat. Japanese varieties will climb up a trellis, pea netting or cane wigwams.

Fennel

'Bulb' formed from swollen leaf bases used like celery, cooked or in salads. Bolts easily if checked by cold or dryness, but new varieties are less prone to this. Fairly hardy.

CONDITIONS Open site, rich, moisture-retentive soil.

GROWING Sow May/early July; best sown *in situ*, but can sow in soil blocks or divided trays provided they are transplanted as soon as they are ready. Mulch and keep well watered.

Garlic

Bulbs from greengrocers can be used for planting, but could give bolting plants and may not be as hardy as named varieties sold for this purpose. In subsequent years save the best bulbs for replanting.

CONDITIONS Sunny position, best on light, rich soil manured for previous crop; good drainage essential.

GROWING Plant individual cloves, choosing the largest, 10–15 cm (4–6 in) apart each way, 4 cm (1½ in) deep. September/October planting gives largest bulbs, as garlic is very hardy and needs a long growing season; however, it can be planted February/March. Lift in late summer when leaves begin to die down, and dry thoroughly. Well grown and harvested bulbs will keep for at least nine months.

Hamburg parsley

A type of parsley with a large swollen tap root; both foliage (like plain-leaved parsley) and root (like a small parsnip) can be used. Hardy – can be left in the ground in winter.

CONDITIONS Sunny or lightly shaded position; moist, fairly rich soil, preferably composted for the previous crop.

GROWING Sow April/May *in situ* in drills 25 cm (10 in) apart and thin seedlings to 13 cm (5 in) or space 15 cm (6 in) apart each way.

Kale

A very hardy brassica; young leaves and shoots most useful in early spring when little else is available. Most varieties have some resistance to clubroot. There are curly and smooth-leaved types. Dwarf forms about 45 cm (18 in) high are best for small gardens and can look attractive, e.g. 'Dwarf Green Curled', 'Ragged Jack'.

CONDITIONS Ideally as for cabbages, but less fussy.

GROWING Sow in a seed bed, soil blocks or trays in April/May. Plant out June to August, dwarf forms 45 cm (18 in), tall forms 60–75 cm (2–2½ ft) apart each way. Dress with blood, fish and bone or seaweed meal in early spring.

Kohl rabi

A quick-growing summer brassica, grown for its swollen stem base; used cooked like a turnip and also good in salads; leaves can be cooked as greens. There are purple and pale green forms. Has some resistance to clubroot.

CONDITIONS Sunny site, best on fertile light soil, not freshly manured, limed if acid.

GROWING Best sown *in situ* March to June, but can be sown in soil blocks or divided trays. Harvest when tennis ball size; late crops can be stored like root crops for winter use.

Lamb's lettuce

A low-growing, leafy salad crop; hardy – most useful in winter and early spring.

CONDITIONS Sunny position; will grow in most ordinary soils, though rich soil is preferable.

GROWING Can be sown at intervals during spring and summer, but usually sown in August for winter use. Sow *in situ* or in rows and thin plants to 10 cm (4 in) each way, or broadcast for a seedling crop.

Landcress

A low-growing salad crop with a hot, watercress flavour. Most useful in winter and early spring – goes to seed quickly at other times.

CONDITIONS Will grow well in light shade (essential for summer crops); moist soil containing plenty of organic matter.

GROWING Sow *in situ*, or in soil blocks or divided trays July/August for winter use. Space plants 15–20 cm (6–8 in) apart each way. Position so that floating mulch (see page 47) can be used if fleabeetle is a problem.

Leeks

One of the most useful hardy winter vegetables. There are early and later (hardier) varieties. A long growing season is required for large leeks, but good yield of smaller leeks can be obtained by closer planting.

CONDITIONS Open site; rich soil, dig in compost or well-rotted manure in winter before planting.

GROWING Sow in seed bed March/April; small numbers can be sown in soil blocks or trays. Plant out May to July when about 20 cm (8 in) tall, in rows 30 cm (12 in) apart, spacing plants 15 cm (6 in) apart, or in blocks with plants 15 cm (6 in) apart each way. Make a hole 15 cm (6 in) deep with a dibber, drop the seedling leek into the bottom and water. Keep well weeded, and when established mulch plants with compost if available.

Lettuce

There are several types: cabbage lettuce, which can be either soft (butterhead) or crisp; long-leaved cos types; and non-hearting types like the decorative 'Salad Bowl' in which individual leaves are picked. Any cos or 'Salad Bowl' type can also be grown as a seedling crop, useful for a quick crop of leaves in spring or autumn. Lettuce can be picked outdoors from late spring to late autumn by using different varieties and sowing times. Choose varieties resistant to root aphid and mildew (like 'Avoncrisp' and 'Avondefiance') if these are a problem. Red varieties can look attractive in flowerbeds.

CONDITIONS Open site, though tolerate light shade in midsummer. Moisture-retentive soil with plenty of organic matter, best manured for the previous crop.

GROWING For an early crop, sow hardy types like 'Little Gem' and 'Salad Bowl' in soil blocks or trays indoors in early March and plant out early April, 23–30 cm (9–12 in) apart in rows 25–30 cm (10–12 in) apart or 23–30 cm (9–12 in) apart each way. Dress with fish, blood and bone or seaweed meal once established. In mild areas, very hardy types like 'Arctic King' can be sown in late August and overwintered to produce a crop about the same time, but they are prone to pest and disease attack.

For main summer/autumn crops, sow and plant out as above, or sow *in situ*, mid-March to late July, every two or three weeks for a continuous supply. Sow hardier types in late July for autumn crops. Water and mulch in dry weather. Germination may be a problem outside in hot weather – sow in blocks or trays in the cool.

For seedling crops, broadcast in patches or sow in close rows from mid April to mid August; seedlings should be about 5 cm (2 in) apart each way. Make first cut when leaves are about 7 cm (3 in) high.

Marrows and pumpkins

Besides the traditional large, stripy marrows and giant orange pumpkins, there are many other types: flat, scalloped custard marrows, spaghetti marrows with flesh that resembles strands of spaghetti, and small nutty pumpkins or 'winter squashes'. There are some bush forms, but most trail and take up a lot of space; however, they can be allowed to romp in an odd space where no other crop would grow and can sometimes be trained up trellises or other supports.

CONDITIONS AND GROWING As for courgettes, but allow 1.2–2 m (4–6 ft) of space each way for trailing types grown on the flat.

Onions and shallots

Main crop onions can be grown from seed or sets. The former keep much better and a much wider range of varieties are available, but they need an early start if large bulbs are to be obtained. Sets are easier and can be put in later, thus often escaping attack by the onion fly. Overwintering onions – modern Japanese varieties or new overwintering sets – give an earlier crop, but may suffer in hard winters and do not store well. Shallots are grown from bulbs; they are useful because they are easy to grow, and store longer than onions. Always buy sets and bulbs from a reliable source to avoid fungal and virus diseases. Salad or spring onions are quick to mature and hardy varieties can be harvested from early spring to late autumn.

CONDITIONS Open site; rich, well-drained soil, manured or composted in the previous winter but never freshly manured.

GROWING **Maincrop onions**: Plant sets early March to early April so that their tips just show above ground; space 5–13 cm (2–6 in) apart in rows 25 cm (10 in) apart or 10–15 cm (4–6 in) apart each way. Bigger spacings give larger onions but less total yield; increase spacings if fungal diseases are a problem. Sow seeds in soil blocks or trays in heat in February/March, or *in situ* in March/April; plant or thin out as for sets. Alternatively sow up to six seeds per soil block; do not thin, and plant out blocks 25 cm (10 in) apart each way; gives clusters of medium-sized onions.

Overwintering onions: Plant sets September/November as for maincrop onions. Sow seeds early August in the north, late August in the south, *in situ* or

Celeriac (see page 57) is easier to grow than celery; the swollen stem base can be chopped or grated for stews or salads

'Ragged Jack' is a dwarf form of kale with a particularly attractive foliage (see page 60)

in soil blocks. Thin in early spring to maincrop spacing and dress with fish, blood and bone or seaweed meal.
Shallots: Plant January to March 15 cm (6 in) apart in rows 23 cm (9 in) apart or 18 cm (7 in) apart each way.
Salad onions: Sow thinly March to June, hardy varieties also July/August, in rows 20 cm (8 in) apart or in bands, spacing seeds 1–2.5 cm ($\frac{1}{2}$–1 in) apart.

Keep all onions well weeded throughout their growing period. Pull salad onions as required. Harvest other onions and shallots as for garlic.

Parsnips
Short types are best for heavy or shallow soils. Varieties 'Avonresister' and 'White Gem' have some resistance to canker.
CONDITIONS Open site; will grow on most soils but best on fairly fertile, deep, light soils, composted for the previous crop.

GROWING Sow March to early May; short types 7.5–10 cm (3–4 in) apart, long types 15–20 cm (6–8 in) apart, in drills 30 cm (12 in) apart, or 10–20 cm (4–8 in) apart each way. A long growing season is required for large roots, but germination is slow and seeds often rot in cold, wet conditions early in the year. Sowing later at the closer spacing can still give good yields.

Peas
Ordinary peas are grouped into earlies, second earlies and maincrop. The first types mature more quickly (in about eleven weeks) and are the best to use early and late in the year and on light soils; in good conditions, maincrop give highest yields. A few varieties, like 'Hurst Green Shaft', have some resistance to mildew. 'Sugar', 'Mange Tout' and 'Asparagus Peas' are all types where the pods are eaten whole while young – many of these types have attractive flowers. Semi-

leafless varieties are best for block sowing on fixed beds as they are almost self-supporting and the lack of leaf allows plenty of air into the block. The roots of peas fix nitrogen in the soil.

CONDITIONS Open site, though can be lightly shaded in summer. Fertile, moisture-retentive, well-drained soil – manure or compost added the previous autumn or put in a trench beneath the row as for runner beans.

GROWING Sow early varieties March/April for first crop, then sow second early or maincrop at intervals from April to mid June. The quick-maturing earlies will also give a late crop if ground becomes vacant for sowing in July. Sow in flat drills 15–20 cm (6–8 in) wide, 5 cm (2 in) deep, spacing seeds 5 cm (2 in) apart with 60 cm (2 ft) between drills. Support plants with pea sticks or netting and mulch between rows. For dwarf or leafless varieties sown in blocks, space seed 10 cm (4 in) each way. Support plants with string and canes round the block.

Potatoes

Varieties are grouped into earlies, second earlies and maincrop. Earlies take up less space, mature most quickly and escape many of the diseases that affect the other types, but yields are lower. Second earlies and maincrop are used for winter storage.

Examples of varieties with some pest or disease resistance are: 'Pentland Javelin', 'Maris Piper', 'Cara' (eelworm); 'Stormont Enterprise' (slugs); 'Maris Piper' (scab); 'Ulster Sceptre', 'Wilja', 'Golden Wonder', 'Estima', 'Stormont Enterprise', 'Maris Peer' (blight). Always buy certified seed potatoes from a reliable source – a greater number of smaller seed tubers are best value. High yields on fixed beds are obtained only at the expense of using many more seed tubers.

CONDITIONS Open site; deep, fertile soil, preferably acid – manure the previous autumn or put compost in trenches (see overleaf).

'Sugar' peas flower prolifically and the pods are deliciously succulent if picked young

New Zealand Spinach is a half-hardy, sprawling plant (see page 64)

GROWING 'Chit' the seed potatoes by putting them in a light, frost-free place until they have sprouts about 2 cm ($\frac{3}{4}$ in) long.

Early varieties: Plant from mid March to mid April in drills or holes 10–15 cm (4–6 in) deep. Space 25–30 cm (10–12 in) apart in rows 38–45 cm (15–18 in) apart or 25 cm (10 in) apart each way on fixed beds (use small tubers or cut large tubers in half). Be prepared to cover emerging shoots with polythene or straw if there are late spring frosts.

Other varieties: Plant 23–38 cm (9–15 in) apart in rows 75 cm (2$\frac{1}{2}$ ft) apart (smaller tubers at the closer spacing) or 30 cm (12 in) apart each way on fixed beds (use small tubers). They can be planted by making individual holes as for earlies; alternatively dig a trench about 30 cm (12 in) deep, put compost or comfrey leaves in the bottom, cover with a layer of soil to 15 cm (6 in) and then plant tubers before filling in remaining soil.

Earth up plants when about 23 cm (9 in) high, or mulch with strawy manure or hay and grass mowings – this is not usually necessary on fixed beds. Watering during dry spells increases yields and can help to control scab disease.

Radishes

Summer radishes can be white or red, round or cylindrical – a useful quick-maturing spring crop, but summer sowings tend to bolt and suffer from pest attacks. Winter radishes can be red or almost black, round or long. They are much larger and will store. The young green seed pods of radishes that have been left to flower can be used in salads.

CONDITIONS Rich, moist soil; open site for spring and autumn sowings, light shade for summer sowings.

GROWING **Summer varieties**: sow *in situ* March to August at intervals in rows 15 cm (6 in) apart or in bands. Thin seedlings to 2.5 cm (1 in) apart. Keep moist.

Winter varieties: sow *in situ* in rows 30 cm (1 ft) apart and thin to 10–15 cm (4–6 in) apart or space 15 cm (6 in) apart each way.

Salsify and Scorzonera

Long root vegetables, not high yielding, that fork on heavy soils, but have a distinctive flavour and do not suffer from as many pests and diseases as most root crops. Very hardy; roots can be left in the soil through the winter, and young shoots from any remaining in spring can be cooked as spinach.

CONDITIONS Open site; deep, rich, light, stone-free soil, not freshly manured.

GROWING Sow April/May in rows 30 cm (1 ft) apart; thin seedlings to 15 cm (6 in) apart or space 15 cm (6 in) apart each way.

Spinach

True spinach is an annual, prone to bolting but useful as a quick-maturing spring or autumn crop. New Zealand spinach is a half-hardy sprawling plant, but it will grow in drier, hotter conditions than other types of spinach. Spinach beet is very hardy – it will usually stand all summer and crop all through a mild winter to give a useful early spring crop before going to seed.

CONDITIONS Tolerates light shade; moist, rich soil best, but New Zealand spinach will succeed in dry conditions.

GROWING **True spinach**: Sow summer types *in situ* March to May, winter types August/September, in rows 30 cm (1 ft) apart, thinning to 15 cm (6 in), or space 23 cm (9 in) apart each way. Keep well watered.

New Zealand spinach: Sow indoors in pots in April and plant out late May or sow outdoors mid May; space 60–90 cm (2–3 ft) apart; a few plants will cover a large area.

Spinach beet: Sow March/April in rows 38 cm (15 in) apart and thin plants to 30 cm (1 ft) apart or space 30 cm (1 ft) apart each way. Can also sow July/August for an extra overwintering crop. Feed with comfrey liquid if plants are not growing well.

Swedes

A hardy root crop in the brassica family; useful for winter storage. The variety 'Marian' has some resistance to clubroot and mildew.

CONDITIONS Open site; light soils containing plenty of organic matter, composted for previous crop, limed if acid.

GROWING Sow *in situ* mid May in north, early June in south, in rows 38–45 cm (15–18 in) apart and thin to 23–30 cm (9–12 in); or space 30 cm (12 in) apart each way. Lift and store before very severe weather.

Swiss chard (seakale beet)

A type of spinach beet with thick white midribs which can be used as a separate vegetable, cooked or in salads. Plants will usually overwinter and go to seed later than spinach beet in spring. Ruby chard is an attractive red-stemmed type, but is more prone to bolting and less hardy.

CONDITIONS AND GROWING As for spinach beet (see opposite).

Sweetcorn

Half-hardy, unlikely to do well in the north, but modern early F_1 varieties are more reliable. Can be undercropped with low-growing plants to save space.
CONDITIONS Sunny, sheltered site; fairly rich, well-drained soil.
GROWING Sow indoors in soil blocks or peat pots in April and plant out when there is no risk of frost. Position in blocks rather than single rows (to help pollination); space 30 cm (12 in) each way for dwarf varieties, 45 cm (18 in) for tall ones. Alternatively, sow *in situ* under jam jars, clear polythene or 'floating mulch' (see page 47). Water and mulch with organic matter in dry conditions. Feed with comfrey liquid if growth poor.

Tomatoes

Half-hardy, best grown with protection in the north. Bush types fruit earlier and can be covered with cloches but slugs may be a problem. Tall types need more attention; they must be staked and side shoots must be taken out, but they produce higher yields in favourable conditions. Fruits can be pink or yellow as well as the traditional red; small, sweet 'cherry' tomatoes like 'Gardener's Delight' and the big fleshy 'beefsteak' varieties are both worth growing as an alternative to the standard supermarket tomatoes. Look through the catalogues for disease-resistant varieties, e.g. 'Ronaclave', resistant to two of the fungal diseases commonly affecting tomatoes.
CONDITIONS Sunny, sheltered site, tall types best against a wall or fence. Well-drained, fertile soil; dig in compost, comfrey leaves or well-rotted manure.
GROWING Sow in pots in gentle heat at the end of March; repot to keep plants growing steadily until planted out when no risk of frost. Space about 45 cm (18 in) apart. Water and mulch – with clean straw for bush types to keep the fruit clean. Feed weekly with comfrey liquid when fruit starts to form, or put fresh comfrey leaves around the base of the plants.

Turnips

A quick-growing root crop in the brassica family, useful for an early summer crop and a late-sown crop for winter use. Tops can be used as spring greens.
CONDITIONS As swedes.
GROWING For an early crop, sow *in situ* March/April, rows 23 cm (9 in) apart; thin to 10–15 cm (4–6 in) apart, or space 15 cm (6 in) apart each way. For winter use, sow July/August *in situ*, rows 30 cm (12 in) apart, and thin to 25 cm (10 in) apart or space 25 cm (10 in) apart each way.

Winter purslane

A low-growing, succulent salad plant, most useful in early spring. Late-sown crops survive mild winters.
CONDITIONS Tolerates light shade; most ordinary soils.
GROWING Sow March to mid August *in situ*, thin plants to 10–13 cm (4–5 in) apart each way.

3
THE
FRUIT GARDEN

The flavour of organically grown fruit from the garden is unsurpassed. This is partly because of its freshness. It is picked when it is ready, not before, and the only journey it has to survive is the one up the garden path. However, its quality is equally a result of the way it is grown – the balanced way it is fed and watered, for example. Variety also plays a part. Garden varieties can be chosen for taste and disease resistance rather than for yield and resistance to rough handling, which are the main considerations of commercial growers.

Producing a succession of homegrown fruit is generally more important than its total yield. The season starts with rhubarb and gooseberries for cooking. Then come strawberries, which carry over into the main summer harvest of raspberries, white and red currants, blackcurrants, dessert gooseberries, plums and cherries. Perpetual and alpine strawberries, autumn fruiting raspberries, blackberries and less familiar berries such as wineberries carry on until the first frost, overlapping with early apples and pears. The latest of these can be picked in November and stored until well into the new year. It is not essential to have an orchard: as this chapter shows, by careful choice of

Opposite: The red currant 'Red Lake' grown as a cordon (see pages 70 and 84)

varieties and growing methods, it is possible to pick fruit throughout the season even in a small garden.

Fruit responds well to natural methods of growing for several reasons. Compost, well-rotted manure and other forms of organic matter provide long-lasting nourishment. They also help to create a well-structured soil in which trees and bushes can grow good roots, making them stable and resistant to drought. Organic fertilizers will provide any additional nutrients necessary, including a wide range of trace elements.

This long-term balanced feeding is most important. Adding too much nitrogen or overwatering causes a lot of leafy growth at the expense of the fruit crop, whereas starving the plant into producing too much fruit detracts from its health. Many sickly symptoms are also caused by a lack or surfeit of certain minerals. In the organic garden it is much easier to strike a happy medium.

Pests and diseases are also less likely to get out of hand. Whereas most vegetables are annuals, fruit trees and bushes remain established for many years. There is therefore less scope for control by rotation and clearing the crop. Continual hygiene in the garden is thus essential – picking up diseased leaves and fallen fruit, and pruning out infected shoots. However, there is also ample chance to achieve a balance between fruit pests and their natural enemies: some of the worst pests of commercial orchards, like red spider mites, usually present no problems to the organic gardener because they are kept under control by predators.

It is, however, essential to get off to a good start by buying suitable varieties. Many modern varieties of soft fruit have successfully been bred to be resistant to certain diseases (mildew of currants and gooseberries, for example), while careful selection of both old and new varieties of tree fruit can help to avoid diseases like scab. Virus infections are common in both soft fruit and tree fruit, symptoms varying from streaked or spotted leaves to marked or distorted fruit. Once infected, the plants cannot be cured even by chemical means and have to be removed. The best way to beat the effects is to purchase healthy plants in the first place – it will generally be a number of years before viruses reinvade.

As explained in Chapter 1, birds are allies in the organic garden – but when currants and berries begin to ripen you may begin to think otherwise! Netted cages and covers are the only really effective way of keeping them off the crop, and here fruit grown against a wall has the added advantage that it can be easily protected. In winter, netting should be removed so that birds can feed on overwintering pests – bluetits, for example, can significantly reduce the number of aphids and codling moth larvae.

Bullfinches will only attack fruit buds when they have exhausted supplies of seeds from other garden plants and surrounding hedgerows – these they find far more satisfying. Some ornamental plants that are good for providing seeds are listed in Chapter 4. Thus an autumn garden which is not *too* tidy can easily be justified. Later in the winter it pays to keep a bird table supplied with suitable feed.

Chemical fertilizers, pesticides and fungicides are certainly not necessary for growing fruit – nor even for getting the best yields. As this chapter shows, there are many more beneficial ways of doing this.

Choosing varieties to suit the growing conditions

Soil

Good drainage and a deep soil are essential conditions for nearly all types of fruit. Only strawberries will grow in a shallow soil, and even then a lot of organic matter must be added to it. The ideal soil is a medium loam, and it is only on such soils that pears and the more temperamental eating apples such as Cox's Orange Pippin succeed well.

Light, sandy or shallow soils can be improved by adding plenty of compost or well-rooted manure so that soft fruit, plums, cooking apples and the more vigorous eating apples can be planted. As we have already seen, manures and fertilizers containing a lot of nitrogen can cause excess leafy growth, so they should only be used in quantity on these poor soils or for fruit such as blackcurrants where a lot of new shoots need to be produced each year. (The specific requirements are given under each individual fruit.)

Heavy clays may need improved drainage and the addition of organic matter such as leafmould or peat to lighten them; afterwards, however, they should give good results for a similar range of fruit – plums, in particular, are tolerant of heavy soils.

Whereas nitrogen has limited applications, potassium is an important nutrient for all types of fruit. Rock potash should be incorporated at the rate of 70–140 g per sq m (2–4 oz per sq yd) – more if there are indications that the soil is deficient in potassium. Typical symptoms of such a deficiency in fruit crops include poor growth and a marginal scorching of the leaves.

Sunshine and shelter

Sunshine affects not only the yield of some fruits but their flavour and colour as well. Pears and gages need the most warmth and shelter, closely followed by late ripening dessert apples. However, cooking apples will tolerate some shade, and cherries, plums and redcurrants can even be planted against a north-facing wall. Raspberries and gooseberries do best in cool but light conditions.

Shelter is important for all types of fruit, partly because wind can cause damage to the leaves, flowers and fruit, but also because pollinating insects are deterred by windy conditions, so the set of fruit is not so good. Pears are particularly prone to wind damage.

Frost

Fruit blossom can easily be damaged by late spring frosts, so in areas where these are likely to occur it is wise to avoid early-flowering varieties or to choose ones that are frost resistant. Most apples come late enough into blossom to escape damage, but the choice of most soft fruit, pears and plums is restricted (examples of varieties are given for each fruit). The other alternative is to provide temporary protection when frost is expected. Strawberries can be covered with cloches or even loose straw, and wall-trained fruit draped with polythene, sacking or netting held away from the blossom with canes. Bushes and small trees can be similarly but less easily protected.

Buying healthy plants

Some viruses cause disease symptoms in fruit while others simply result in poor growth and reduced yields – effects that it would be easy to blame on the soil or a lack of fertilizer. Either way, plants that are free from virus are more vigorous and produce more fruit of better quality.

Such plants can readily be obtained from nurseries that are in the Ministry of Agriculture's plant certification scheme. Most of their stock will have been propagated from virus-free plants that were obtained from one of the government research stations. The propagation areas of the nurseries are inspected by the Ministry during the growing season each year and the stock certified as healthy and true to type. It should now be possible to obtain virus-free plants of most new summer-fruiting strawberries, most raspberries, hybrid berries, blackcurrants and even rhubarb, together with a wide range of apples, pears, plums and cherries, both old and new.

Even if what you are looking for is not available as virus-free stock, it is still best to buy the plants from specialist nurseries where standards are high. It is just not worth accepting gifts of strawberry runners, raspberry canes and currant and gooseberry cuttings over the garden fence, nor buying bushes and trees from market stalls.

Making the most of limited space

The main factors that influence the size of a fruit tree or bush are the variety, the way it is pruned and trained, the fertility of the soil and, in the case of trees, the rootstock.

Varieties that are not too vigorous and whose growth is upright rather than spreading are obvious choices for the small garden – the blackcurrant 'Ben Sarek', for example.

Good use can be made of walls and fences by training cordons, fans or espaliers against them. Gooseberries, red and white currants, apples, pears, plums and cherries can all be grown in one or more of these forms. Apples, pears and plums can also be pruned into free-standing 'dwarf pyramid' trees which take up relatively little space.

Cultivated varieties of tree fruits are not grown on their own roots but are grafted onto 'rootstocks', which make a big difference to their eventual size. Recently introduced dwarfing rootstocks for apples, plums and cherries make it possible to grow free-standing trees in a very small garden – though they are not always the best choice for planting on poor soils where growth is already less vigorous. Trees on dwarfing rootstocks start to bear fruit at a much earlier age.

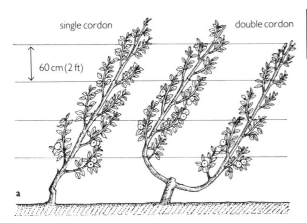

single cordon   double cordon

60 cm (2 ft)

a

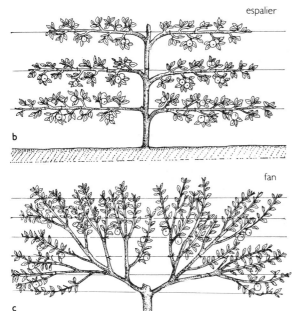

espalier

b

fan

c

Mixing fruit and ornamental plants

There is no need to set aside a special plot for fruit in a small garden: it can be ornamental as well as functional. Alpine strawberries can be used as edging and among shrubs; blackberries and other hybrid berries can be trained along wires to make an attractive screen between one part of the garden and another, as can espalier apples and pears. Redcurrants and gooseberries can be grown like standard roses. If well pruned, fruit trees make a positive contribution to the appearance of the garden even when they are not in flower or bearing fruit.

The fruit also benefits from not being isolated. Ornamental plants can attract pollinating bees and other beneficial insects in summer, and in winter provide cover and food for birds.

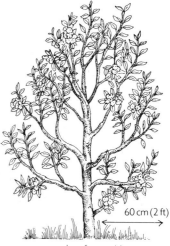

60 cm (2 ft)

dwarf pyramid

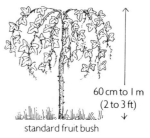

60 cm to 1 m
(2 to 3 ft)

standard fruit bush

(a) **Cordons** consist of single straight stems along which fruit is borne on short spurs. They are usually trained at an angle of 45 degrees, which gives more length and encourages fruiting. Apples, pears, red and white currants and gooseberries can be grown as cordons
(b) **Espaliers** usually have two or three tiers of outstretched horizontal arms about 45 cm (18 in) apart. Apples and pears are suitable for growing in this form
(c) **Fans** make the best use of wall space: they need horizontal wires about 23 cm (9 in) apart so that the shoots can be tied in evenly over the whole area. Plums, cherries, apples, pears, red and white currants and gooseberries all do well when fan-trained

Dwarf pyramids are very compact, with a central stem about 2.3 m (7 ft) high from which branches radiate almost all the way up. Apples, pears and plums can be grown in this way

Standard fruit bushes give height in an ornamental bed and make picking easy. Red and white currants, gooseberries and worcesterberries can be grown in this way

Checking pollination requirements

Many fruit trees will not produce a good crop unless their flowers are fertilized with pollen from a different variety. This is the case with most apples, many pears and some plums. Even a variety that is 'self-fertile' often produces a better crop if another variety is planted nearby – close enough for bees to carry the pollen from one to another. Usually any two varieties that flower at the same time will pollinate each other, but there are exceptions. Fruit nursery catalogues usually indicate with a number or letter the flowering time of each variety, and list combinations that are incompatible.

Planting more than one tree in a small garden can be a problem, which is why cordons are so suitable. Another way out is to grow a 'family tree', which consists of a collection of varieties (usually about three) grafted on to one rootstock. The varieties should be carefully chosen to ensure that they will cross-pollinate each other and that their growth is evenly balanced. Nevertheless, careful pruning is essential.

A young fruit tree being trained as a fan growing at the back of a mixed border of flowers, herbs and vegetables at Ryton Gardens. Note the generous mulch to conserve water and suppress weeds

Planting

Most fruit trees and bushes are dug up from nursery beds and sold with bare roots rather than in containers. They can be planted at any time between November and March when the weather is suitable, though the earlier the better. Their initial healthy growth depends a great deal on how well they are planted.

The ground should be prepared beforehand by digging and by the addition of organic matter and fertilizers as indicated in Chapter 1. Prepare the whole area if a number of bushes or a row of cordons or raspberries is to be planted, and at least 1 m (3 ft) square for individual trees or plants against walls. Then dig out a hole for each, and plant as described in Chapter 2. For trees it is most important that the graft with the rootstock is at least 10 cm (4 in) above the surface. If a tree needs support, drive a stake in on the windward side of

the tree before filling in the hole so that you can position it near the trunk without damaging the roots.

Pruning

Pruning is one of the most important operations in fruit growing, and has particular significance in the organic garden because it is a good non-chemical way to help increase yields and reduce pest and disease damage.

The time to prune and the exact method are different for nearly every type of fruit and each form of tree or bush, and it is worth getting a specialist book on the subject, particularly if you are training young fruit trees. This chapter can only cover briefly the methods of pruning for established stock. However, it always helps to know why pruning is necessary and what its effects are.

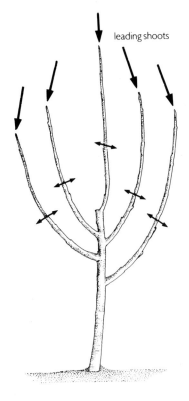

leading shoots

The effect of pruning a bush when it is dormant (left) is to stimulate vigorous new growth just below the cut (above). Note that the new shoots grow in the direction in which the dormant buds were pointing

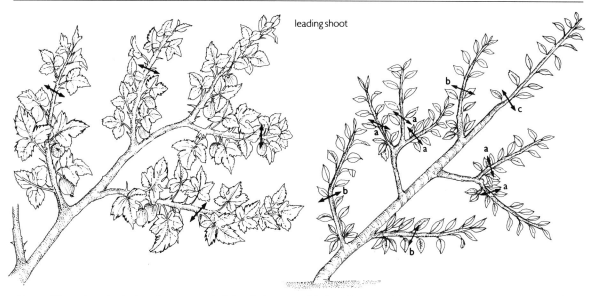

leading shoot

Above: **Gooseberries** In late June to early July all the side shoots produced that season should be trimmed to five leaves, to encourage fruit buds to form. Then in winter the leading shoot is cut back
Right: **Cordon apples** Summer prune mid July to early August.

(a) Cut shoots arising from existing side shoots to one leaf beyond the cluster at the base **(b)** Cut all side shoots longer than 23 cm (9 in) growing directly away from the main stem to three leaves beyond the cluster of leaves at the base **(c)** If cordon has reached its final height, cut back to 2.5 cm (1 in)

There are three basic reasons for pruning:

- To shape the bush or tree, both when it is young and being trained into shape, and to maintain it when established.
- To encourage the formation of fruit buds so that more fruit is produced.
- To help control pests and diseases.

Pruning is traditionally thought of as a winter occupation, but a lot of pruning is in fact best done in summer, particularly that of dwarf fruit trees and those trained against walls.

Shaping the tree

Winter pruning stimulates growth, because the root system of the tree or bush has been established during the previous summer to feed its full complement of branches. When spring comes and the energy is redistributed, the buds below the cuts grow rapidly. Thus winter pruning the 'leading' shoots is important for building the new framework of a young plant.

Summer pruning has the opposite effect: removing shoots when they are in full leaf takes energy away from the plant and limits its growth. It is thus an effective way of keeping vigorously trained trees and bushes in shape. Pruning in summer is also much more pleasant than tackling the same task with chilled fingers in winter, and pruning cuts heal quickly, with less chance of disease entering the wound. Obviously, though, trees that are making poor growth should not be summer pruned. Nor should those such as blackcurrants, which bear most fruit on one-year-old wood.

Encouraging fruit buds

The vigorous growth that results from winter pruning is sometimes produced at the expense of the fruit crop, whereas summer pruning can stimulate fruiting. For example, trees and bushes often bear fruit on short 'spurs' close to the main stem: red and white currants, gooseberries, and many (but not all) varieties of apples and pears behave like this. Such fruiting spurs can be encouraged to form by pruning back in summer the lateral shoots growing from the main stems.

Helping to control pests and diseases

Judicious pruning is one of the best defences against fruit diseases. The first stage in pruning any tree or bush should be to cut out dead or infected wood before the infection spreads: this applies to coral spot on currants and canker on apples, for example. Aphids and mildew on the shoot tips of gooseberries and redcurrants can be directly removed by summer pruning. It is, of course, essential to clear up all infected prunings and burn them.

The aim of both winter and summer pruning is then to thin out the branches, removing any that are rubbing or crossing, and in some cases to tip back side shoots so that light and air can reach all parts of the plant. The crowded conditions under which fungal diseases flourish should never occur if careful pruning is carried out.

Pruning cuts

Pruning cuts should be made at points close to a branch or buds, or the shoots tend to die back. Use sharp tools and make clean cuts, as these heal quickly and minimize the risk of disease entering the tissues. Where possible, cuts should be made at an angle so that they shed water quickly.

Small cuts less than 2.5 cm (1 in) in diameter made in this way should not need any protective coating to help them heal. Many 'wound paints' on the market contain chemicals, and there is some evidence to show that they actually hinder the healing process. For larger cuts a 'biological' material can be painted on. This takes the form of a powder, made up into a paste or liquid, which contains the beneficial fungus *Trichoderma viride* (page 36) which attacks any disease fungi that try to penetrate. Alternatively, liquid animal manure painted onto the wound may give some protection by providing nourishment for the beneficial fungi that are naturally present.

Weeding, watering and feeding

It is easy to see if weeds are strangling a vegetable crop; their effect on fruit trees and bushes is not so obvious. However, weeds and grass will in fact reduce the growth and yield of fruit – mainly because they compete for water. This is most noticeable in the first year or two after planting.

Mulching is by far the most appropriate form of weed control, as it also helps to conserve moisture and avoids the risk of damaging the fibrous roots that many types of soft fruit make near the soil surface. A long-lasting mulch is a good investment on weedy land: black plastic, compressed peat paper, cardboard or newspapers held down with old grass mowings, will all keep perennial weeds down for at least one growing season (see page 30). Provided that any organic matter and fertilizers required for the specific crop are dug in before planting, no additional feeding should be necessary during this time. By the second or third year all perennial weeds should have disappeared, and an annually renewed loose mulch of straw, compost or manure should be sufficient. Any fertilizers that are necessary can be raked in before the mulch is put down in late spring. Seaweed meal is one of the most useful of these, as it contains readily available potassium.

Regular watering is essential for any fruit trees or bushes in the first summer after they have been planted. Established plants suffer a loss of yield and have smaller fruit in dry conditions, but too much water produces soft growth liable to fungal infection, and fruit that lacks taste. Again it is a question of striking a balance. The time when water is most critical is just after the fruit begins to swell – this is also the time when new growth is being made to support next year's crop. Plants on light soils and those planted against walls are particularly vulnerable, and may need more regular watering. Water should always be given in large doses – say 9–18 litres (2–4 gal) at a time for each tree or bush.

Strawberries

The large strawberries picked by the bowlful in June and July could never be replaced, but there are other types useful to the amateur gardener: the less vigorous 'perpetual' or 'remontant' strawberries, which have similar but smaller sweet berries; and alpine strawberries, which have tiny berries with a delicate, aromatic flavour. Both these types fruit in irregular flushes throughout the summer until the autumn frosts.

Situation

Strawberries need a sunny site, except for alpine varieties, which will grow in light shade. The soil must be well drained, ideally slightly acid (pH 6.0–6.5), and not compacted – so raised beds are particularly suitable. Plenty of well-rotted manure or compost should be added, together with about 70 g per sq m (2 oz per sq yd) of bonemeal and a similar amount of seaweed meal.

Because of soil-borne pests and diseases, summer and perpetual strawberries should not be grown for more than three or four years in any one place. It is often convenient to fit them in with the crop rotation in the vegetable garden, or rotate them with annuals in a sunny border. Alpine

Strawberries growing through a black 'woven' plastic mulch (see page 30)

STRAWBERRY VARIETIES

Variety	Cropping period	Disease resistance	Yield
RED GAUNTLET	Early mid summer; does well under cloches	Resistance to mildew and grey mould	Heavy cropper
CAMBRIDGE FAVOURITE	Mid summer; fruits last well	Resistance to mildew	Crops well under a wide range of conditions
SALADIN	Mid summer	Resistance to grey mould and mildew	Heavy cropper
TROUBADOUR	Late mid summer; flowers avoid spring frosts	Resistance to mildew and verticillium wilt	Less yield but useful for extending the season
AROMEL	Perpetual (Aug-Oct)	More susceptible to mildew and virus	Less yield than summer varieties
MARASTAR	Perpetual (Aug-Oct)		

strawberries, with their attractive leaves and compact growth, can be used as an ornamental plant: edging a rose bed, grown beneath shrubs, or planted in spaces between paving stones.

Recommended varieties

Many varieties of summer fruiting strawberry exist, but only a few are widely available. New varieties are generally less susceptible to virus and fungus disease (see chart on page 75). Their flavour is sometimes questioned but growing them organically will make all the difference. Alpine strawberry varieties differ from one another in the size of their fruit and whether or not they make runners – nearly all are good.

Planting

Plant from July to September: the later the planting, the less the yield the first year. Those planted in spring should have the flowers taken off so that they do not fruit that summer. Put in the plants firmly, with the crowns just sitting on the surface, not buried. Space summer varieties 38–45 cm (15–18 in) apart in rows 75 cm (30 in) apart; other types 23–30 cm (9–12 in) apart.

After-care

Plants can be kept free of weeds by shallow hoeing: spread straw around them just before the fruit ripens to keep it clean. Alternatively, plant through black plastic (500 gauge should last three to four years) or black woven ground cover material (see page 30). Cut off new runners thrown out by the plants to concentrate their energy on fruiting. Immediately summer varieties have finished cropping, cut off the old leaves about 7.5 cm (3 in) above the crown, as if left these will only weaken the plant. Sprinkle seaweed meal round the plants in early spring.

STRAWBERRY PESTS AND DISEASES		
Pest/disease	**Symptoms**	**Prevention**
BOTRYTIS	Grey mould on berries, especially in wet weather.	Keep fruit dry by strawing: do not overcrowd plants.
POWDERY MILDEW	Leaves turn purple; fruit loses shine.	Use resistant varieties; grow in an open site; do not overcrowd plants.
VERTICILLIUM WILT	Outer leaves wilt; young leaves yellow and small.	Avoid planting strawberries after potatoes; grow resistant varieties.
VIRUS DISEASES	Blotched and crinkled leaves, stunted plants, poor crop.	Use new varieties and buy certified stock; dig up and burn affected plants; spray against aphids.
RED SPIDER MITE	Bronzed leaves; weakened plants.	Generally kept under control by predators.
SLUGS	Eat holes in fruit, especially in wet weather.	Keep fruit dry by strawing.
APHIDS	Colonies infest new growth; can spread virus disease.	Spray with derris or insecticidal soap.
EELWORMS	Feed on roots, causing stunting and distortion of plant.	Rotate crops; buy certified stock.

Raspberries

Most raspberry varieties are summer fruiting — they produce berries sometime between the end of June and mid-August, on canes that grew the previous year. There are also a few autumn-fruiting varieties, which fruit on the current season's canes; these have a much lower yield but are useful for extending the season where conditions are good.

Situation

Raspberries grow best on deep, light, slightly acid soils (pH 6.0–7.0). They need plenty of water but good drainage. On limey soils iron and manganese deficiency may occur, showing as yellowing of leaves between the veins. To prepare the ground, fork in plenty of well rotted manure or compost to two spades' depth and add rock potash if necessary (see page 24).

A sheltered site in full sun will give the best yields, but summer-fruiting varieties will grow in light shade. All summer-fruiting raspberries need support from posts and wires and are usually planted in rows, which could be used to form a temporary summer screen. Rows running north to south will cause less shading. In a small garden a few plants (up to ten canes) can be trained up a single post. Autumn fruiting varieties, which are less vigorous, may not need support and could be grown in a clump in a wilder part of the garden.

Recommended varieties

The varieties in the table (below) are chosen for their range of cropping times, disease resistance and flavour; as with strawberries, the flavour depends very much on how they are grown.

Planting

Plant any time from November to March when conditions are suitable, but November is best. Space canes 38–45 cm (15–18 in) apart in the rows, and cut them back to 30 cm (12 in) directly after planting. The top roots of the canes should be 5–7.5 cm (2–3 in) below the soil surface. Allow 1.5–2 m (5–6 ft) between rows.

RASPBERRY VARIETIES

Variety	Cropping period	Disease resistance	Characteristics
MALLING JEWEL	Early	Tolerant of virus infection.	Compact growth; reliable if not heavy cropper.
GLEN MOY	Early	Resistance to aphids.	Reputedly good flavour.
GLEN PROSEN	Mid-season	Resistance to aphids.	Reputedly good flavour.
MALLING ADMIRAL	Mid-season	Good overall health.	One of the best varieties if only one is grown — good for eating fresh, freezing and jam.
LEO	Late	Some resistance to aphids and to cane spot and spur blight.	Heavy cropping; upright canes.
SEPTEMBER	Autumn	(traditional variety)	Much lower yields than summer varieties.
ZEVA	Autumn	(new variety, good for colder areas)	

Autumn-fruiting raspberries are less vigorous than summer-fruiting varieties

After-care

The fruiting canes of summer raspberries are usually supported by a single line of posts and wires, or trained into a 'V' on two wires. The latter system allows the new canes to grow up between the old ones during the summer without fear of being damaged, and separating the two sets of canes can also help to prevent fungus diseases.

In late spring scatter seaweed meal along the rows at a rate of 70–140 g per sq m (2–4 oz per sq yd) and mulch them heavily – old hay or straw is ideal for this, not manure unless the soil is very poor. Leave space immediately round the canes for the soft new canes to emerge. A trickle hose along the row is ideal for providing the moisture that raspberries need, without wetting the foliage and encouraging disease.

RASPBERRY PESTS AND DISEASES

Pest/disease	Symptoms	Prevention
SPUR BLIGHT	Purplish blotches around nodes on canes, extending and turning silvery white in winter. Yield much reduced.	Cut out and destroy affected canes. Use resistant varieties and ensure that the soil is well drained. Do not overcrowd canes. Train as in Figure F6.
CANE SPOT	Small, round, purple spots on new canes, turning elliptical and grey. Most prevalent where rainfall is high.	
BOTRYTIS	Grey mould on berries; in bad cases affects the canes, which turn a purplish grey.	Do not overcrowd canes or water overhead with a sprinkler. Do not overfeed plants.
VIRUS DISEASES	Yellow mottling or blotching and distortion of leaves. Loss of vigour and yield.	Dig out and burn infected plants. Use resistant varieties.
RASPBERRY BEETLES	Eggs laid in the flowers; these hatch into small white grubs that tunnel into the berries as they ripen.	Spray with derris when the first pink fruit is seen.
APHIDS	Cause distortion of young leaves; spread virus diseases.	Spray with derris or insectidal soap. A few varieties have some resistance to attack.
EELWORMS	Cause loss of vigour; spread virus diseases.	Do not replant new raspberries in old beds.

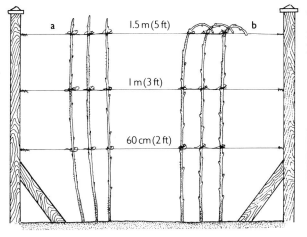

Train summer-fruiting raspberry canes on a single line of wires stretched between 2 m (6½ ft) high posts. Space the canes 7.5–10 cm (3–4 in) apart. Tie them individually or lace them to the wire with a continuous piece of twine. Then either **(a)** cut canes to a bud above top wire, or **(b)** cut off the top 15 cm (6 in) and loop the canes over to form a series of arches

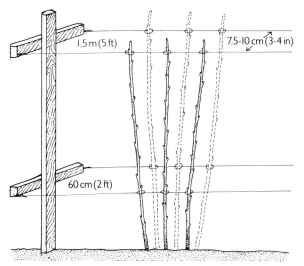

Training raspberries on two wires so that new canes can grow up between them.

Pruning

The canes of summer varieties that have borne fruit should be cut out completely when the crop has finished. The number of new canes should be reduced so that there is one to every 7.5–10 cm (3–4 in) of wire. Cut autumn-fruiting canes back to soil level each winter.

Blackberries and less familiar berries

Although there may be blackberries in the hedge-rows, there are still advantages to growing a plant or two in the garden. The cultivated forms have bigger fruit which ripen earlier and are easier to pick (some varieties are thornless); they are attractive to look at and bees love the flowers. Both blackberries and the less common hybrid berries such as loganberries, tayberries and boysenberries are more tolerant and disease resistant than raspberries and yet can be used in similar ways – for cooking, freezing, as jam and fresh with cream. Although they are vigorous plants they can sometimes occupy space that is not useful for anything else. Those most suitable for small gardens are described in the table overleaf.

Situation

Like raspberries, all these berries like a well-drained soil and plenty of organic matter, but their need for nitrogen is greater because of the large amount of new cane they must produce. Thus manure and hoof and horn (about 112 g or 4 oz) should be forked into each planting hole.

The plants need considerable support, and are therefore usually trained on wires against a wall or fence. Blackberries could be used to sprawl over eyesores like old pipework, or could be woven into an informal hedge. They crop best in a sunny place but will give some fruit in partial shade and fairly cold conditions – against a north or east wall, for example. The flowers come late and are therefore not susceptible to frost damage.

RECOMMENDED TYPES OF BLACKBERRY AND HYBRID BERRIES	
BLACKBERRY Ashton Cross	Most like a wild blackberry but bigger fruit. Space needed 3.7 m (12 ft).
Oregon Thornless	Less rampant, has very attractive cut leaves, and fruit of good flavour. Space needed 2 m (6 ft).
LOGANBERRY	The familiar blackberry/raspberry cross; thornless varieties are available. Space needed 2.5 m (8 ft).
BOYSENBERRY	Large purplish/black berries with a flavour of their own; moderate growth; a thornless variety available. Space needed 2.5 m (8 ft).
TAYBERRY	Like loganberries but darker and larger; moderate growth; thorny. Space needed 2.5 m (8 ft).

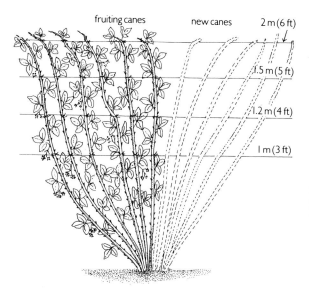

Training blackberries and hybrid berries on a single line of wires and posts

Planting

Plant at any time from November to February, the earlier the better, at a depth so that the small white shoots at the base of the old canes are only just below the soil surface. Most plants need about 2.5 m (8 ft) of wall space.

After-care

The canes should be fanned out and tied or woven into wires. Using only one half of the fan for the fruiting canes allows the new canes to be tied in the other direction as they grow during the summer, reducing the danger of any fungal diseases spreading to them.

Mulch the base of the plants in late spring – use manure or add seaweed meal if the canes are not growing vigorously enough to fill their alloted space.

Pruning

Cut out old canes in autumn after they have finished fruiting, and cut the weak tips off the new canes.

Pests and diseases

In theory, these berries can be affected by the same pests and diseases as raspberries, but they are less susceptible to nearly all of them, including virus diseases and botrytis. Raspberry beetle is usually the worst problem (see page 78).

Blackcurrants

Blackcurrants bear the most fruit on wood which is only one year old, and this has a great influence on how they are grown and pruned. It makes them less economic in terms of space than many soft fruits, but some of the new varieties form compact bushes which give a high yield without sacrificing any of the fruit's distinctive flavour. It is particularly important to buy certified bushes (see page 69) to ensure that they are free from reversion virus, which is the most serious blackcurrant disease.

RECOMMENDED BLACKCURRANT VARIETIES	
All these varieties are compact enough to grow in a small garden. Their blossom escapes or can withstand frost, and they have good resistance to mildew and leaf spot.	
SEABROOK'S BLACK	Early/mid-season; has some resistance to big bud.
BEN SAREK	A new variety, very compact, only 1–1.1 m (3–3½ ft) high, and bushes need only be spaced 1.2 m (4 ft) apart.
BEN LOMOND	Slightly later flowering; high yield; large berries.
MALLING JET	Late flowering and ripening, thus extending the season; often recommended for eating raw.

Situation

Blackcurrants are more tolerant of heavy soils than many soft fruits, but any site must be well drained. Dig in plenty of manure or compost to retain moisture and encourage the growth of new shoots on which fruit buds will be formed. Add hoof and horn at a rate of 140 g per sq m (4 oz per sq yd) unless the soil is very fertile.

The way blackcurrants grow and fruit makes them unsuitable for growing against walls. Bushes should be in full sun to do well, and should not have competition from grass or other plants. They really need a place of their own, but could be grown in an open mixed border.

In frost-prone areas, choose late-flowering varieties or ones whose blossom can withstand damage (see table below).

Planting

Plant any time from November to February, but preferably in late autumn. In general allow 1.5 m

BLACKCURRANT PESTS AND DISEASES

Pest/disease	Symptoms	Avoidance/control
REVERSION VIRUS	Poor growth, much reduced yields. Flower buds bright purplish red, and leaves with fewer veins than healthy bushes.	Dig up and burn infected bushes. Buy certified stock. Control big bud mites (see below) which spread the disease.
MILDEW	White powdery coating on leaves.	Use resistant varieties. Try elder or urine sprays (see page 36).
LEAF SPOT	Dark brown spots on leaves. Whole leaves turn brown and drop in wet summers.	Avoid susceptible varieties. Clear up and burn infected leaves.
BIG BUD MITE	The mites are tiny, but the buds they are feeding within become bloated compared to healthy ones – this is easiest to see from January to March.	Pick off and destroy affected buds: delay pruning until January so that badly affected branches can be chosen for removal.
CURRANT APHIDS	Several types attack blackcurrants in spring. Young leaves become distorted. Sooty mould forms on lower leaves.	Predators are often sufficient to keep them under control on established bushes, until they move to other plants in summer. If new growth is seriously affected, spray with quassia or insecticidal soap.

(5 ft) between bushes (see table). They should be put in about 2.5 cm (1 in) deeper than they were in the nursery to encourage new shoots to come right from soil level. After planting, prune each branch back to a few inches of growth or to two buds above soil level.

After-care

Mulch bushes in late spring, preferably with farmyard manure or compost. Top up the mulch with lawn mowings during the summer.

Pruning

About one-third of the old wood should be cut out from each bush every winter. Start by taking out weak, damaged or crossing branches, and ones that droop near the ground; then select a few old, strong shoots for removal. Make all cuts as near as possible to the base of the bush to encourage new growth to come from here.

Gooseberries and worcesterberries

Gooseberries may be more trouble in the organic garden than many soft fruits, because whole bushes can be ruined by sawfly caterpillers and many varieties are badly affected by mildew (see opposite). However, they otherwise grow well, suffering little from virus diseases (only new varieties like 'Invicta' are available as certified stock). They are ready early and have a long picking season; they are usually classified as 'dessert' or 'cooking' gooseberries, but many cooking varieties are good for eating raw if they are left on the bushes to colour and ripen. The worcesterberry is a species closely related to the gooseberry and should be treated in a similar way.

Situation

Gooseberries grow best on a light, well-drained

RECOMMENDED VARIETIES OF GOOSEBERRY

Variety	Ripening time	Type of fruit	Characteristics
INVICTA	Early to mid-season	Culinary; pale green berries.	Very good mildew resistance, but vigorous prickly bush, in a small garden best grown as a cordon.
LANCASHIRE LAD	Mid-season	Dual purpose; large, dark red berries.	Some mildew resistance; high yielding, upright bush.
CROWN BOB	Mid-season	Dual purpose; large, dark red berries.	Some mildew resistance; spreading bush.
GOLDEN DROP	Mid-season	Dessert; small yellow berries.	Upright, compact bush.
WHITESMITH	Mid-season	Dual purpose; large, pale green berries.	Vigorous, upright bush.
WORCESTERBERRY	Mid-season	Culinary; small, dark red berries.	Vigorous bush, very good mildew resistance.

soil which contains plenty of organic matter and is slightly acid (pH 6.5–7.0). However, they are more tolerant of a heavy soil than raspberries. Add compost or well-rotted manure to poor soils, but otherwise gooseberries should not be overfed – too much lush growth encourages mildew and aphids. They flower early, so frost damage can be a problem, and they need a sunny sheltered site to yield well.

Gooseberries fruit year after year on short spurs along the length of their branches, so these can be trained into a permanent framework: as fans or cordons along a wall or screen (see page 70) and as ornamental standards (see page 70) as well as ordinary bushes.

Planting

Plant any time from November to February, but preferably in November. Give bushes plenty of space – about 1.5 m (5 ft) each way – so that the prickles can be avoided when picking. Single cordons should be spaced 30–45 cm (12–18 in) apart, double cordons 60–90 cm (2–3 ft), and triple cordons or fans about 1 m (3 ft); insert canes alongside the cordon branches. They should be planted at the same depth as in the nursery and any buds at the base of the stem rubbed off.

After-care

In late spring mulch with old hay or straw to keep down weeds and retain moisture. Established plants should make about 15–23 cm (6–9 in) of new growth each year; if they are not growing strongly, sprinkle seaweed meal at a rate of 140 g per sq m (4 oz per sq yd) around them before the mulch is applied.

Pruning and training

Gooseberry bushes should ideally be pruned in summer and winter. In late June to early July prune all the new lateral shoots to five leaves (see page 73). Pull off any suckers that arise from the base of the bush. In winter, cut back the leading shoots by one half to a bud facing in the required direction (upwards in varieties with weeping branches) and cut out crowding and crossing branches. Cut the laterals that were pruned in summer back further to two or three buds.

Cordons and fans are pruned in much the same way: lateral shoots should be pruned in summer and winter; new leading shoots should be tied to the canes pointing in the required direction and cut back in winter to half their length until the cordons have reached the required height – then cut them back to leave only 1 cm ($\frac{1}{2}$ in) of new growth.

Winter pruning can be carried out at any time from November to March. If birds eating the buds is a problem, late pruning is preferable since by then they will be moving on to other food and the shoots can be cut back to undamaged buds.

GOOSEBERRY PESTS AND DISEASES

Pest/disease	Symptoms	Prevention/control
AMERICAN GOOSEBERRY MILDEW	White powder on shoot tips and later on leaves, stems and berries. Can seriously affect yield and growth.	Do not use susceptible varieties. Cut off mildewed shoot tips when summer pruning. Try elder or urine sprays (see page 36).
APHIDS	Grey-green aphids infect shoots in spring.	Remove tips of shoots in summer pruning. Spray with derris or insecticidal soap.
GOOSEBERRY SAWFLY	The sawfly caterpillars (green with black heads and spots) feed on leaves and can quickly reduce them to skeletons.	Keep a close watch on bushes; pick them off by hand or spray with derris before numbers build up.

Redcurrants and white currants

Red and white currants may not be such popular fruit but they are easy to place in the garden and rarely suffer badly from pest or disease attacks. Few certified plants are available as they are not badly affected by viruses, but it is still wise to buy them from a good nursery. Redcurrants are particularly suitable for making jelly and wine and mixing with blackcurrants in puddings. White currants are delicious raw in fruit salad when they are really ripe.

Situation

Both red and white currants like similar growing conditions to gooseberries but have the advantage that they will crop well in a shady place. They can be trained as bushes (on a 'leg', like gooseberry bushes), as standards, or as cordons and fans. As their requirements are less exacting than those of blackcurrants, a red or white currant bush could be grown among ornamental shrubs; fans or cordons can even be grown against a north wall.

Planting and after-care

Currants should be treated in the same way as gooseberries. Their growth is similar, the branches forming a permanent framework with fruiting spurs, but with the advantage that they are easier to train into a well-shaped, manageable bush – and there are no prickles!

Rhubarb

Rhubarb is not botanically a 'fruit' because it is the leaf stalks that are harvested. Nevertheless, in practice it is a useful spring crop as early varieties can be forced for harvest as soon as March, and it is relatively trouble-free to grow (see opposite).

Situation

Rhubarb needs a well-drained, sunny position, but will grow on any type of soil provided that plenty of manure or compost has been dug in. In such conditions the plants grow very large; if there is space for them they can look attractive as part of a flower border. If drainage is a problem, they are best grown on a raised bed.

RECOMMENDED CURRANT VARIETIES

There is little to choose between varieties in taste and appearance – the following varieties are hardy and suitable for growing in a small garden.	
RED LAKE	Mid-season; one of the commonest varieties, moderately vigorous.
RONDOM	Late-season; good for exposed and cold gardens.
WHITE VERSAILLES	Mid-season; widely available, recommended for eating raw.

PESTS AND DISEASES OF CURRANTS

Pest/disease	Symptoms	Avoidance/control
CURRANT 'BLISTER' APHID	Red blisters on leaves in early summer, starting at shoot tips.	Summer prune shoot tips. Mature bushes can usually withstand attacks until the aphids migrate to other plants in late summer. If young bushes are severely attacked, spray with quassia or insectidal soap.
CORAL SPOT	Branches die back and coral-coloured growths appear on the dead wood.	Cut out affected branches several inches below the dead wood and burn them.

Planting

Plants can be set in at any time from October to March, 75–90 cm ($2\frac{1}{2}$–3 ft) apart with the buds just above soil level. Some varieties can be grown from seed; sow in spring in a seed bed or in pots and plant out into permanent positions the following spring.

After-care

Mulch with a thick layer of manure or compost each spring. The large leaves quickly swamp most weeds around them, but be careful not to let perennial weeds become established in the crowns.

After midsummer the leaves should be left unpicked so they can build up the roots that will feed next year's crop. By then the stalks will have lost their flavour because the amount of oxalic acid in them will have increased – in large quantities oxalic acid is poisonous.

In autumn, when the leaves have died down, cover the crowns with a layer of leafmould or straw several inches thick.

RECOMMENDED VARIETIES OF RHUBARB	
TIMPERLEY EARLY	One of the very earliest varieties; slender stalks, red at base; virus-free plants available.
PRINCE ALBERT	Early; bright red stalks; virus-free plants available.
GLASKIN'S PERPETUAL	Mid-season; stalks rather green but low in oxalic acid; can be grown from seed.

DISEASES OF RHUBARB		
Disease	Symptom	Control
CROWN ROT	Fungus causes crowns to rot away.	Dig up and burn affected plants; replant new stock in another place.

Apples

There are a bewildering number of apple varieties available, and sampling shop-bought fruit is not a true indication of their taste. Early varieties suffer in transit and later ones are often put straight into cold store and never allowed to mature. Even the notorious 'Golden Delicious' picked straight from the tree really *is* delicious! The other considerations in choosing apples are their hardiness, pollination requirements, disease resistance and cropping times. Only a selection of all the varieties worth considering has been given overleaf.

Situation

Apples ideally need a sunny, sheltered site and a deep, well-drained, loamy soil – and many eating varieties will do well only in such conditions. However, cooking apples will crop in partial shade and are more tolerant of heavy soils. Light, sandy soils must have plenty of well-rotted manure or compost dug in and then cookers or the more vigorous eaters can be grown. Depending on the soil, fork in 140–280 g per sq m (4–8 oz per sq yd) of rock potash and 70–140 g per sq m (2–4 oz per sq yd) of bone meal before planting. On cold sites, choose hardy, late-flowering varieties.

Espaliers, fans and cordons can be grown against a sunny fence or wall or, on sheltered sites, along a post and wire framework (espaliers look particularly attractive like this). Dwarf trees can be planted in lawns or borders, but must be kept free from competition from grass or other plants (see below). Trees are often available on three or four different rootstocks, and cordons on two (see overleaf). The new very dwarfing rootstocks are useful for small gardens, but the more dwarf the tree, the more care it needs: it must be staked all its life, and fed and watered more often.

Planting

Plant at any time from November to March when conditions are suitable. Space bushes according to

RECOMMENDED APPLE VARIETIES

COOKING VARIETIES	Pollination group (see page 71)	Eating time	Comment
REV. W. WILKS	2	Aug-Nov	Small tree, good for small gardens.
ARTHUR TURNER	3	Aug-Oct	Scab resistant. Upright growth, good tree for small gardens.
GRENADIER	3	Aug-Oct	Good resistance to canker and scab.
GOLDEN NOBLE	4	Sept-Jan	Vigorous, disease free; also good eaten raw.
NEWTON WONDER	5	Dec-March	Vigorous, scab resistant and very hardy.
EDWARD VII	6	Nov-March	Flowers late, thus suitable for frosty areas.
CRAWLEY BEAUTY	7	Dec-Feb	Flowers late, and very hardy, thus good for cold places; scab resistant.
EATING VARIETIES			
DISCOVERY	2	Aug-Sept	Sweet, crisp, red fruit. Frost-tolerant blossom and scab resistant.
SUNSET	3	Oct-Dec	Small, yellow, Cox-like fruit. Scab and mildew resistant.
WINSTON	4	Jan-March	Small yellow fruit, scab resistant.
JUPITER	4	Oct-Feb	Vigorous; Cox-like fruit but will flourish where a Cox will not.
LORD LAMBOURNE	5	Nov-Dec	Pale green/red aromatic fruit; compact tree; good resistance to scab, mildew and canker.
KING OF THE PIPPINS	5	Oct-Dec	Yellow russetted fruit; high yielding; scab resistant.
AMERICAN MOTHER	5	Oct-Dec	Small aromatic fruit; vigorous; scab resistant.
COURT PENDU PLAT	6	Dec-May	Flowers late, so misses frost; small fruit; compact tree, good in adverse conditions.

APPLE ROOTSTOCKS

Variety	Character	Suggested use	Spacing of bush trees
M27	Extremely dwarfing	Small gardens on fertile soils, vigorous varieties.	1.2–2 m (4–6 ft)
M9	Very dwarfing. Bushes 2–3 m (6–10 ft)	Small gardens on fairly good soil, widely used.	2.5–3 m (8–10 ft)
M26	Dwarfing. Bushes 2.5–3.7 m (8–12 ft)	Small gardens on poorer soil, less vigorous varieties. Also used for pyramids, cordons, espaliers and fans on good soil.	3–4.5 m (10–15 ft)
MM106	Trees 3.7–5.5 m (12–18 ft)	Larger gardens on a wide range of soils. Recommended for cordons, espaliers and fans on most soils.	3.7–5.5 m (12–18 ft)

'Discovery', a crisp eating apple

rootstock (see opposite), cordons 75–90 cm ($2\frac{1}{2}$–3 ft), espaliers 3.5–4.5 m (12–15 ft), fans 3.0–4.5 m (10–15 ft) and dwarf pyramids 1.5–2 m (5–7 ft). Use the closer spacing for less vigorous varieties on poorer soils. Trees on dwarfing rootstocks M27 and M9 will need permanent stakes.

After-care

An area of at least 1 m (3 ft) square around each tree should be kept free of grass and weeds by mulching with old straw or hay, for example, or using mulching mats (see page 31). Every few years (more often on poor soils or if the tree is not making good growth) use compost or well–rotted manure, and apply about 140 g per sq m (4 oz per sq yd) seaweed meal in early spring. The mulch will also help to retain moisture, but apples need regular watering in dry periods, especially those on the dwarfing rootstocks.

Apples are subject to many pests and diseases, and conventional orchards are frequently sprayed as a matter of course. However, as table on page 88 shows, as well as encouraging natural predators there are many preventive measures that can be taken in the organic garden.

Pruning established trees

Cordons

Once the cordon has reached the required height, cut back the growth on the leader to 2.5 cm (1 in) each July. Summer prune the laterals as described on page 73 in the third or fourth week in July (the further north you are, the later you should prune).

Espaliers and fans

When the 'arms' have reached the required length, cut them back to 2.5 cm (1 in) in July and summer prune each as if it were a cordon.

APPLE PESTS AND DISEASE

Pest/disease	Symptoms	Avoidance/control
SCAB	Leaves have olive green blotches. Brown or black scabs form on fruit and shoots. The fungal spores overwinter on dead leaves. Favoured by wet weather.	Grow varieties with some resistance. Prune out scabby shoots. Sweep up fallen leaves or chew them up with a lawn mower so that they are taken under more quickly by worms.
MILDEW	White coating of delicate threads and powdery spores on leaves and young shoots, turning silvery in winter. Severe in warm, humid conditions.	Do not grow susceptible varieties like Cox and Golden Delicious. Prune off any 'silvered' shoots in winter, and remove any that are badly infected if they are spotted early in spring. Dilute urine spray (3:1) may help.
CANKER	Splits and craters form in bark; if these girdle a shoot or branch then it will die. Often made worse by poorly drained soils. Infection enters through cuts in the bark, but can also come through leaf scars if leaves drop when the weather is wet. Vigorous leafy growth makes the trees susceptible.	Avoid susceptible varieties like Cox. Make sure site is well drained and do not use manure on fertile land. Cut out small shoots and branches that are affected, and cut scarred tissue out of larger ones (treat cuts with Trichoderma powder – see page 36). Remove autumn leaves of small young trees by hand on a dry day and avoid damaging bark.
APPLE SAWFLY	Maggots tunnel into the developing fruits, leaving holes with debris round them; these fruits fall by mid summer and maggots pupate in the ground.	Pick off infected fruit before they fall if possible, and do not leave them on the ground. Spray with derris at petal fall.
CODLING MOTH	The main cause of maggoty apples! The larvae burrow into the fruit in late summer and they drop to the ground four to six weeks later. They often pupate and overwinter in crevices in the bark.	The larvae have many natural predators among insects (earwigs, for example) and birds (bluetits are estimated to take 95 per cent of overwintering larvae). Some larvae can also be trapped by tieing sacking or corrugated cardboard bands around the branches in July where they can pupate; the bands are then taken off and destroyed during the winter.
APPLE APHIDS	Colonies develop on young shoots in spring and can cause curled leaves and distortion of fruit. Eggs overwinter in bark crevices.	Spray shoots with derris or insectidal soap. Encourage birds like bluetits in winter.
WOOLLY APHIDS	Cause galls on woody stems.	Has many natural predators, so not usually a problem in an organic garden.
RED SPIDER MITE	Colonies cause bronzing of leaves and they fall early.	Has many natural predators, so not usually a problem in an organic garden.
CAPSID BUGS	Eat ragged holes in leaves and damage blossom.	Difficult to control organically, but damage usually not severe.
WINTER MOTH	Brown or green 'looper' caterpillars feed on opening buds and young leaves. They drop to the ground in June, pupate in the soil, and the wingless females climb back into the trees in winter.	Spray with Bacillus thuringiensis in spring when caterpillar damage is seen. Put a band of fruit-tree grease (a special vegetable grease) round each tree trunk in October and renew throughout the winter – this catches the returning females.

Dwarf pyramids

In winter, prune the central leader to leave about 23 cm (9 in) of new growth, cutting to buds on alternate sides each year, until the tree has reached the required height. Then cut back the new growth to this point each summer. Maintain the pyramid shape by removing any vigorous upright shoots, and summer pruning each of the side branches as if it were a cordon.

Dwarf bush trees

Once the framework of branches has been formed, pruning should only be light unless growth is weak. Keep the bush open by cutting back to about 10 cm (4 in) lateral shoots that grow into the centre, and cut out any branches or laterals that have become overcrowded.

Many common apple varieties are 'spur-bearing' and their fruit buds can be encouraged to form by cutting back laterals not needed for the framework to four or five buds in winter. Conversely, tip-bearing varieties produce most buds at the tips of shoots made the previous summer. Thus all new lateral shoots less than 23 cm (9 in) long should be left unpruned. Longer laterals can be cut back to four buds in winter to encourage new, shorter ones to form.

Pears

Pears are not as easy to grow as apples, and in anything other than ideal conditions it is essential to choose one of the hardier varieties (see below). A few varieties give some fruit without help from another pollinating variety, but all give better crops if they are cross-pollinated.

Situation

Pears need the same deep, fertile, slightly acid soil as dessert apples, and should be given similar treatment. Sunshine is also important and shelter essential. They flower early, so on frost prone sites grow cordons or fans against a sunny wall where they can be protected.

RECOMMENDED PEAR VARIETIES

Variety	Pollination group (see page 71)	Eating time	Comment
JARGONELLE	3	Aug	Long fruit, good flavour. Hardy and scab resistant. Needs two pollinators.
DR JULES GUYOT	3	Sept	Large yellow fruit. Scab resistant. Sets some fruit without a pollinator.
CONFERENCE	3	Oct–Nov	Long, slender fruit, firm white flesh. Hardy and fairly vigorous but needs to be sheltered from the wind. Will crop without a pollinator but the fruit are often misshapen.
FERTILITY IMPROVED	4	Oct	Round yellow russetted fruit; heavy cropper, disease resistant. Sets some fruit without a pollinator.
WINTER NELIS	4	Nov–Jan	Small, juicy, aromatic fruits. Small tree. Blossom fairly frost tolerant.
CATILLAC	4	Dec–March	Hard fruit for stewing. Vigorous, high-yielding tree. Blossom fairly frost tolerant. Needs two pollinators.

Dwarf pyramid pears are more widely available than pyramid apples and these, or bush trees, can be planted in lawns and borders on sheltered sites. There are only two rootstocks suitable for a small garden (see below).

Planting

Plant any time from November to March when conditions are suitable. Space bushes according to rootstock (see below), cordons 60–90 cm (2½–3 ft), fans 3–4.5 m (10–15 ft) and dwarf pyramids 1.5–2 m (5–6 ft) apart.

After-care

Like apples, pears need a weed-free area around them. However, their requirement for nitrogen is greater, and they should be fed with seaweed meal (about 140 g per sq m–4 oz per sq yd) and mulched with well-rotted manure each spring. They suffer from a number of troublesome fruit pests and diseases against which avoidance measures can be taken, and they are also susceptible to fire blight (see below).

Pruning

The growth of pears is less rampant and more upright than that of many apples, and nearly all pears bear fruit on spurs. Bush, pyramid and wall-trained trees and cordons should all be pruned in the same way as apples, but summer pruning should be carried out earlier, starting in early July in the south.

PEAR ROOTSTOCKS

Variety	Character		Suggested use	Spacing of bush trees
QUINCE C	More dwarfing	but final height of tree depends more on variety than on rootstock	Trees on very good soils or very vigorous varieties	3–4.3 m (10–14 ft)
QUINCE A	More vigorous		Suitable for wider use	3.5–4.5 m (12–15 ft)

PEAR PESTS AND DISEASE

Pest/disease	Symptoms	Avoidance/control
CANKER	See apple canker	See apple canker
SCAB	See apple scab	See apple scab
FIRE BLIGHT	Leaves turn brown and leathery but remain on the tree; branches die back.	Any suspected infection must be reported to the local Ministry of Agriculture. If confirmed tree must be dug up and burned.
APHIDS	See apple aphid	See apple aphid
PEAR LEAF BLISTER MITE	Brown blisters on leaves in summer caused by burrowing mites.	Pick off and burn infected leaves.
PEAR MIDGE	Larvae feed in young fruit which blacken and fall. They then pupate in the soil.	Collect and destroy infected fruit as soon as it falls. Fork soil between affected trees in winter to expose pupae to birds and frost.

Plums, gages and damsons

As with apples and gooseberries, there are varieties of plums suitable for eating raw and others for cooking (see overleaf). 'Gages' are types of dessert plum that are particularly sweet and juicy. Damsons are a hardier, less vigorous type of plum, with a strong, distinctive flavour, very good for puddings and jam.

Some varieties of plum are self-fertile, so one only need be planted in a small garden.

Situation

Plums need plenty of moisture and organic nitrogen but must not be waterlogged. They are fairly tolerant of heavy soils, but plenty of rotted manure or compost must be dug into light ones. Lime must be added to acid soils.

All plums flower early, so a sheltered site that escapes late frosts is essential. Dessert plums and gages need a warm, sunny position to ripen properly and are best trained as a fan on a south or west wall. Cooking plums need less sun and can also be grown on an east wall – a few even on a north wall – or in the open. Damsons are much hardier than plums; they will grow in colder places and are less troubled by frost or wind. They could be planted in a hedgerow to provide a windbreak for other fruit trees.

In the open plums and damsons are usually grown as bush trees, but they can be trained as dwarf pyramids. The recently introduced dwarfing rootstock Pixy is the best for small gardens,

'Marjorie's Seedling is a late flowering and large fruiting plum

RECOMMENDED PLUM VARIETIES

DESSERT VARIETIES	Eating time	Comment
EARLY TRANSPARENT GAGE	Mid Aug	Self-fertile, hardy. Pale yellow fruit with almost a greengage flavour.
DENNISTONS SUPERB GAGE	Mid-late Aug	Self-fertile, vigorous, hardy (suitable for north or east wall). Large, pale green fruit.
VICTORIA	Aug-Sept	Self-fertile, vigorous, hardy (suitable for north or east wall). Pale red fruit, also good for cooking. Susceptible to silver leaf.
SEVERN CROSS	Sept-Oct	Self-fertile. Large, deep yellow fruit with a good flavour.
COOKING VARIETIES		
CZAR	Aug	Self-fertile, vigorous, very hardy with good frost resistance (suitable for north wall). Dark purple fruit.
BELLE-DE-LOUVAIN	Aug	Self-fertile, vigorous, hardy (suitable for north wall), upright growth. Purple fruit with a rich flavour.
MARJORIE'S SEEDLING	Late Sept-mid Oct	Self-fertile, vigorous, upright growth. Late flowering, so often escapes frost damage. Large blue/black fruit.
DAMSONS		
SHROPSHIRE OR PRUNE DAMSON	Sept-Oct	Self-fertile, hardy, compact growth. Small blue/black fruit.

PLUM PESTS AND DISEASE

Pest/disease	Symptoms	Avoidance/control
SILVER LEAF	Leaves have a silvery appearance and branches progressively die back. A purplish stain is produced in the wood.	Do not prune plum trees in winter, and treat all large pruning wounds with *Trichoderma* powder. Inoculate infected tree with *Trichoderma* pellets (see page 36).
BACTERIAL CANKER	Long scars which exude gum; leaves on affected branches are small and yellow.	Prune out badly affected branches.
VIRUS DISEASES	Fruit of poor quality. Low yields.	Dig up and burn affected trees. Buy virus-free stock.
APHIDS	Colonies of leaf-curling aphids build up on young shoots.	Snip off those shoots badly affected when they are first seen. Spray with quassia or insectidal soap.
RED SPIDER MITE	Bronzing of leaves.	Natural predators usually control outbreaks in an organic garden.

especially on good soils. It gives compact trees only about 2.5 m (8 ft) high, which can crop in the third year after planting. It has better anchorage than dwarf apple rootstocks but is still more susceptible to drought. On poor soils, the semi-dwarfing rootstock St Julian A is suitable for fans and pyramids.

Planting

Plant any time from November to March when the weather is suitable. Space bushes or fans on Pixy 3–3.5 m (10–12 ft) apart and on St Julian A 3.7–4.5 m (12–15 ft) apart. Space pyramids on either rootstock 3–3.5 m (10–12 ft) apart.

Trees in the open will need staking for the first five or six years, and sometimes permanently on exposed sites.

After-care

As with apples and pears, plums must be kept free of competition from weeds and grass, as they need to make good growth. Mulch with farmyard manure in late spring. Water during dry spells, particularly fan-trained trees near walls and trees on Pixy rootstocks.

Plums generally suffer less from pests than apples and pears and the main disease, silver leaf, is one for which there is a good organic remedy: the beneficial fungus *Trichoderma viride* is used as a 'biological control'. This remedy is even used by non-organic commercial growers (see table on page 36).

Pruning

Plums are usually pruned in early spring when growth has just started, or summer pruned later in the growing season. Cuts should never be made in winter, when they are slow to heal, because of the risk of silver leaf infection.

The fruit is borne on short spurs on two-, three- and four-year-old wood and on growth made in the previous summer. A proportion of older wood that has become bare with age may need to be cut out each year as the tree gets older.

Bush trees

Established trees need little pruning. Usually all that is necessary is to cut out dead, broken or crossing branches in July and August.

Dwarf pyramids

In May, shorten the new growth on the leading shoot to 2.5 cm (1 in) once it has reached the required height. In late July, shorten the new growth of each branch to eight leaves – always to a downward facing bud – and the laterals from it to six leaves. Cut out any vigorous shoots growing upwards at the top of the tree.

Fans

In early spring, as growth begins, rub out shoots growing into the wall or directly away from it. In July, pinch back new shoots not wanted for the framework to six or seven leaves. In autumn, cut these back to three leaves to make fruiting spurs.

4
FLOWERS AND SHRUBS

Ornamental plants often take second place in the organic garden, where growing healthy fruit and vegetables is so important. They may well be given little room – and that principally in places where nothing edible will grow! But, as we have seen, they do have a significant role to play.

All the more reason, then, why they should be chosen carefully. They must give good value for space, with long-lasting flowers, scent, leaves or stems that look attractive when the flowers have gone, seedheads or berries in autumn. They should also be hardy, relatively easy to care for, and not susceptible to pest and disease attack. Fortunately, there are plenty of plants that satisfy these demands, as the rest of this chapter will demonstrate.

A few modern shrubs and flowers have been bred with resistance to certain diseases, and some ornamental shrubs have been propagated from virus-free stock – but on a far smaller scale than for fruit and vegetables. It is usually native plants and their closely related garden varieties that are hardiest and most disease resistant; highly developed strains, selected for qualities like enormous flowers or unusual colour, are often far less robust.

Staking flowers can be very time-consuming, so chose varieties that are short and sturdy, or that

Opposite: Flowers that attract beneficial insects have an important place in the organic garden

sprawl naturally without looking untidy. Not all shrubs need expert pruning – some just need the occasional trim, and in a few cases even this is not essential.

Planting for wildlife

Another criterion for choosing ornamental plants is their ability to attract wildlife to the garden. Those that provide food – pollen, nectar, seeds or berries – immediately bring an extra dimension to the garden: the steady hum of bees, the elusive charm of butterflies and the entertaining sight of finches feasting on seedheads.

Flowers advertise what they have to offer by their colour and scent. Long-tongued bees, for example, are attracted to blue and purple flowers like cornflowers, which often have nectaries only they can reach. Hoverflies, on the other hand, favour flat, open flowers like yarrow, where the nectar is easily accessible. Pale, fragrant flowers which open at night, such as evening primroses, attract moths.

Plants that bloom in early spring – like wallflowers and the many spring-flowering bulbs – are particularly valuable for newly emerging insects. Similarly, the late flowers of Michaelmas

RECOMMENDED ANNUALS AND BIENNIALS

Name	Type	Height	Flower type/ flowering time	Growing conditions	Comment
ALYSSUM (*Alyssum maritimum*)	Half-hardy annual (but hardy in the south)	7.5–15 cm (3–6 in)	Usually white; May-Sept; sweet honey scent.	Ordinary soil, full sun.	Good for edging; loved by bees; fleabeetle may attack seedlings.
CHERRY PIE (*Heliotropium × hybridum*)	Half-hardy annual	30–45 cm (12–18 in)	Mauve; July-Sept; sweet 'cherry' scent.	Fairly fertile soil, full sun.	One of the best annuals for butterflies.
CORNFLOWER (*Centaurea cyanus*)	Hardy annual	30–60 cm (1–2 ft)	Blue/purple/white; June-Sept.	Ordinary soil, full sun.	Grow the native blue type if possible.
EVENING PRIMROSE (*Oenothera biennis*)	Biennial	60–90 cm (2–3 ft)	Pale yellow, open at night; June-Oct; strongly scented.	Well-drained soil, sunny position.	Attracts night-flying moths.
FORGET-ME-NOT (*Myosotis* species)	Biennial	20–30 cm (8–12 in)	Blue; March-June.	Moist soil, partial shade.	Native – avoid refined garden varieties. Suffers from powdery mildew in dry conditions.
FOXGLOVE (*Digitalis purpurea*)	Biennial	1–1.2 m (3–4 ft)	Purple, pink or white; June-Aug.	Moist soil, partial shade.	Native – avoid refined garden varieties.
HONESTY (*Lunaria biennis*)	Biennial	60–75 cm (2–2½ ft)	Purple; April-June.	Any well-drained soil; sun or partial shade.	Good early nectar plant. Orange-tip caterpillars feed on leaves. Seed pods attractive and loved by finches.
MIGNONETTE (*Reseda odorata*)	Hardy annual	30–38 cm (12–15 in)	Cream; July-Sept; strongly scented.	Any ordinary soil; sunny position.	Good for bees and some butterflies.
MARIGOLD (*Calendula officinalis*)	Hardy annual	30–60 cm (1–2 ft)	Bright orange; May-Oct.	Will grow in poor soil; sunny position.	Good for hoverflies; seeds for birds in autumn. Powdery mildew can affect plants in dry conditions.
PETUNIA (*Petunia × hybrida*)	Half-hardy annual	15–30 cm (6–12 in)	White/pink, mauve/blue; June-Oct.	Ordinary well-drained soil; sunny position.	Grow 'multiflora' types with smaller, less delicate flowers. Single varieties useful for pollen and nectar.
POACHED EGG PLANT (*Limnanthes douglasii*)	Hardy annual	15 cm (6 in)	White with yellow edges; May-June from early sowings or self-sown seeds.	Ordinary soil; sunny position.	Useful edging plant, good early flower for bees and hoverflies.
SUNFLOWER (*Helianthus annus*)	Hardy annual	1–3 m (3–10 ft)	Golden yellow; July-Sept.	Well-drained soil. Add compost for giant types.	Provides nectar for bees and butterflies, and seeds in autumn.
SWEET WILLIAM (*Dianthus barbatus*)	Biennial	15–60 cm (6–24 in)	Dark red or pink with white markings; June-July; richly scented.	Any well-drained soil; sunny position.	Good for early pollen and nectar – one of the best butterfly plants.
TEASEL (*Dipsacus fullonum*)	Biennial	1–2 m (3–6 ft)	Blue/mauve; July-Aug.	Moist soil; sunny position.	A native; flowers visited by bees and butterflies; seedheads popular with goldfinches.
TOBACCO PLANT (*Nicotiana* species)	Half-hardy annual	60–90 cm (2–3 ft)	White/pink/mauve; June-Sept; highly scented when open at night.	Well-drained, composted soil; warm sheltered position; sun or light shade.	Attracts night-flying moths.

daisies allow insects to build up energy for their winter sleep.

In all cases, choose the simple, original varieties rather than frilly new hybrids where pollen and nectar are hidden beneath a dense cluster of petals, or not produced at all. Plant all flowers in bold groups of the same type rather than dotting them around the garden – this makes a more eye-catching display and also suits the habits of nectar-seeking insects. The most useful plants are those whose flowers are followed by seeds or berries: yarrow, for example, produces a good seed crop for birds and the heads do not look unattractive if left in the flower border.

There are also many less noticeable forms of wildlife that can be encouraged – a whole collection of insects and other tiny creatures that are less entertaining but equally important in the organic garden. They help to make up the natural, balanced community of pests and predators in which no one pest can multiply to 'plague' proportions. They also form the basic diet of larger garden inhabitants such as hedgehogs and bats.

Unlike the birds and bees, to whom your colourful border of exotic flowers can be a banquet, many of these creatures are very limited in what they eat, and may depend entirely on a few native plants. While it is impossible to satisfy each of these selective creatures, any native flower or shrub will almost always support a wider range of insects than an exotic one – another reason, besides their hardiness, for using them in the garden wherever possible. In fact many do make attractive garden plants: what could be better than the sight of primroses and pasque flowers in spring, for example, or the red stems of dogwood in winter?

Many native shrubs and trees are of course far too vigorous for small – or even large – gardens. However, they can often be kept to manageable size by planting them in a mixed hedge which is cut annually: hawthorn, buckthorn, field maple, hazel, elder, holly, wild privet, spindle, guelder rose and even some large tree species such as oak can all be used like this.

Caring for ornamental plants

As with fruit and vegetables, the essence of growing ornamental plants organically is to understand how they grow, so each can be given the conditions it needs in order to flourish. The scope for choosing the right plant for the right place is much greater for flowers and shrubs, however. For example, spring bulbs can flourish under deciduous trees where it is dry and shady in summer, but never where it is wet; there are, on the other hand, shrubs and herbaceous plants that will tolerate waterlogged conditions.

Most are not fussy whether the soil is acid or alkaline, but there are exceptions even among common plants: many heathers, rhododendrons and azaleas, for example, will grow only in an acid soil.

In general, ornamental plants do not demand a lot of nutrients. A soil that is too rich can cause too much leafy growth at the expense of flowers. Manure and fertilizers containing a lot of nitrogen are therefore usually inappropriate; poor or heavy soils are best improved using well-rotted compost, leafmould or peat. Bonemeal is the most useful fertilizer, particularly for plants that stay in the ground for many years, like naturalized bulbs, shrubs and roses.

A mixture of shrubs, herbaceous plants, bulbs and seasonal flowers is the best way of satisfying the growing conditions in a garden, and providing colour and interest throughout the year. It is also the best for wildlife, as the several tiers of vegetation create habitats for a whole range of creatures. Shrubs give the garden its height and shape, and shelter flimsier plants from strong winds. The evergreens are important for winter colour and for providing a dry, dense cover for birds, hedgehogs and other small mammals. The flowers of deciduous shrubs add to the ever-changing scene, and their canopy provides a 'woodland' atmosphere for shade-loving plants. In a small garden, climbing plants trained on fences, trellises or posts make a good substitute for this higher layer of growth. Below, herbaceous plants and low-growing shrubs form the basis of the seasonal displays of colour, with annual flowers and bulbs filling in the gaps.

Mulching in spring will take care of annual weeds, but it is essential to clear the ground of perennial weeds *before* planting: removing the roots of dandelions and docks from among a stand of bulbs, or the stems of bindweed from flimsy herbaceous plants, is almost impossible! Leafmould, peat, bark or woodchips all make attractive mulches that show off ornamental plants well – and also create another 'layer' of wildlife activity.

An ornamental bed can then almost look after itself, though just a little regular attention will make all the difference to its appearance. Cutting off faded flowerheads in early summer can help to prolong the display of some annuals and

perennials, and removing diseased leaves helps to prevent the spread of fungal diseases. Overgrowth of shrubs should be trimmed back every year at the appropriate time, not left until it requires major surgery. General tidiness, however, should always be tempered by the needs of other creatures in the garden: save some seedheads for birds, dry stalks for sheltering ladybirds and leaves for hibernating hedgehogs, for example.

Pest and disease control largely relies on growing healthy, vigorous plants that can overcome most attacks. Damage of the right sort is usually more tolerable on ornamental plants than on edible produce: nibbled leaves of mature plants often do not spoil their flowers, for example, and the appearance of the striking yellow and green mullein moth caterpillar is almost worth the sacrifice of a ragged plant! However, there are a few devastating pests and diseases of flowers and shrubs which it is wise to look out for, and these are described in the following sections.

Annuals and biennials

Annuals are plants that grow from seed, flower, set seed and die all in one season; 'hardy' annuals are those that can be sown directly outside in the ground, and these often seed themselves; half-hardy annuals must be raised in the warm and planted outside. Biennials grow from seed to form a rosette of leaves during their first summer; this overwinters, then the plant completes its life cycle and dies the next summer; biennials also often self-seed.

Although annuals and biennials can be a little more trouble to grow than perennials, they can provide quick colour in the garden. Often seeds of a hundred or more varieties are available in garden centres, so it is easy to experiment with different types from year to year if you want to. Many are

Opposite: Mixed annuals grow successfully in any well-drained soil

Left: The seedheads of teasel are favoured by goldfinches and the flowers attract butterflies

RECOMMENDED BULBS

Name	Height	Flower type and flowering time	Planting time/ depth	Situation
BLUEBELL (*Endymion nonscriptus*)	23 cm (9 in)	Blue (though there are white and pink varieties); April-June.	Aug-Sept (as soon as available); 10–13 cm (4–6 in)	Moist but well-drained soil with plenty of organic matter; sun or light shade; will naturalize under trees and in summer-sown grass or borders; where possible use this native species rather than the 'Spanish bluebell', which is also widely available.
CROCUS (Dutch) (*C. vernus* hybrids)	7.5–12.5 cm (3–5 in)	Gold/purple/white; March.	Sept-Oct; 7.5 cm (3 in)	Any well-drained soil; best in full sun; will naturalize in short grass or borders.
CYCLAMEN (*C. hederifolium*)	7.5–10 cm (3–4 in)	Mauve/pink/white; Aug-Nov; attractive patterned leaves.	Aug-Sept; 2.5–5 cm (1–2 in)	Well-drained soil containing plenty of organic matter; shady position: will grow in the dry, bare area around the base of trees or shrubs. This is one of the most useful species of hardy cyclamen, although there are several others that flower at different times.
DAFFODIL AND OTHER NARCISSI (*Narcissus* species)	Dwarf vars. 15 cm (6 in); tall vars. 30–45 cm (1–1½ ft)	Yellow/orange/white; March-May depending on variety; 'jonquils' and some 'poeticus' narcissi are scented.	Aug-Sept. Depth three times the height of the bulb (see page 102)	Fairly fertile, well-drained soil; sun or partial shade. The wild daffodil *Narcissus pseudonarcissus* is available from some specialist nurseries.
FRITILLARY (*Fritillaria meleagris*)	23–30 cm (9–12 in)	Chequered white and purple, or pure white; April-early May.	Sept-Nov; 10–15 cm (4–6 in)	Fairly fertile, moist but well-drained soil, sunny position. Will grow in fine, late-cut grass but probably best in borders. A rare native plant; not easy to establish but well worth it.
GRAPE HYACINTH (*Muscari* species)	20 cm (8 in)	Usually blue; April-May.	Sept-Nov; 7.5 cm (3 in)	Any well-drained soil; best in full sun; use in flower beds or for edging but not in grass. A common flower which spreads quickly, but a favourite with bees and butterflies.
LILY-OF-THE-VALLEY (*Convallaria majalis*)	15–20 cm (6–8 in)	White, sweetly scented; April-May; red berries in autumn.	Sept-Oct; 2.5 cm (1 in)	Soil containing plenty of organic matter; partial shade; will tolerate dry conditions; a rare native plant but common in gardens.
MEADOW SAFFRON (*Colchicum autumnale*)	15 cm (6 in)	Mauve; Sept-Nov.	July-Sept; 10 cm (4 in)	Well-drained soil containing plenty of organic matter; sun or light shade. Best planted in rough grass (stop mowing August to late spring) as leaves are untidy in borders. Native.
SNOWDROP (*Galanthus nivalis*)	13 cm (5 in)	White with green markings; Jan-March.	Just after flowering if possible; 10 cm (4 in)	Fairly fertile, moist but well-drained soil; light shade. Will naturalize in short grass or under trees. This is the native (or long naturalized) species, useful for very early flowers.
SQUILL (*Scilla* species)	7.5–10 cm (4–5 in)	Blue; March.	Oct; 5–7.5 cm (2–3 in)	Moist but well-drained soil, sun or light shade. Will naturalize in short grass or under trees.
STAR OF BETHLEHEM (*Ornithogalum* species)	20–30 cm (8–12 in)	White with green markings; April-May.	Oct; 5 cm (2 in)	Any well-drained soil. Sun or light shade. Will naturalize in late-mown grass or under trees. *O. nutans* and *O. umbellatum* are native (or long naturalized) species, readily available.
TULIP (dwarf) (*Tulipa greigii*)	12–25 cm (5–10 in)	Mainly red; April.	Nov; 15 cm (6 in)	Any well-drained soil; sunny, sheltered position. This is one of the best dwarf tulips (there are other species); will naturalize in borders.
WINTER ACONITE (*Eranthis hyemalis*)	7.5–10 cm (3–4 in)	Yellow; late Jan-Feb.	Aug-Sept; 2.5–5 cm (1–2 in)	Moist but well-drained soil; sun or light shade. Will naturalize in short grass or under trees or shrubs. This is the commonest and earliest flowering species, naturalized in the wild in some places.
WOOD ANEMONE (*A. nemerosa*)	15–20 cm (6–8 in)	Commonly white but there is a blue form; March-April.	Sept-Oct; 3–5 cm (1½–2 in)	Fairly fertile, well-drained soil; sun or very light shade. A native plant of open woodland: will naturalize among shrubs.

the old-fashioned scented 'cottage garden' flowers that bees and butterflies love, such as mignonette, sweet williams, foxgloves and canterbury bells.

Situation

Most annuals and biennials will flourish in any well-drained soil without the addition of compost or fertilizers; peat or leafmould can be used to improve badly structured soils. Most also prefer a sunny position, though there are some that will grow in moist, shady places. Annuals and biennials are useful for filling in gaps between newly planted shrubs and herbaceous plants, or taking over when spring bulbs have finished; they take little from the soil and therefore do not deprive the other plants of nutrients. They also fit in well with the annual rotation on vegetable plots and can be grown as a bright edging, either just for fun or to attract beneficial insects like hoverflies; a few, like nasturtiums, provide tasty leaves for salads.

Sowing and planting

Annual flowers should be sown directly into their growing positions. This is usually done in spring, but some are hardy enough to be sown in autumn in sheltered areas, and these will give early blooms the following year. They can be broadcast in patches or sown in a series of short drills (see page 21), and later thinned to the required spacing. Half-hardy annuals must be sown inside in early spring – or bought from a nursery or garden centre – and planted out in early summer when there is no longer any risk of frost.

There are no strict rules for spacing – plants can be anything from 15 cm (6 in) apart for small, delicate ones to 60 cm (2 ft) for large, bushy ones. Obviously closer planting gives a mass of colour more quickly, but larger plants can become drawn if they are too crowded, and the risk of fungal diseases is increased.

After-care

After initial hoeing and hand weeding, the plants need little care. Remove faded flowerheads during the summer where possible to help keep the plants blooming, but remember to leave some of the hardy types to self-seed and attract birds in autumn; the whole dead plant should be removed in winter or early spring.

Annuals and biennials do suffer from a few specific pests and diseases – such as fleabeetle and clubroot which affect those in the brassica family (see page 111), but attacks are not usually devastating if the plants are grown in the right conditions. If the worst comes to the worst, individual plants that become badly affected are dispensable and can be put onto the compost heap. Slugs are often the most damaging pest and sometimes seem to be just waiting for their annual feast of bedding plants! Individual lemonade bottle 'cloches' (see page 32) are the only reliable answer to this problem.

Bulbs

Bulbs are plants with storage organs below ground. Botanically they can be separated into true bulbs (like daffodils), corms (like crocus), tubers (like dahlias) and rhizomes (like lily-of-the-valley). However, they all grow in similar ways and will be treated as one group here. Although the familiar spring-flowering bulbs are the most useful, both for early colour and as food for insects when little else is available, there are hardy summer- and autumn-flowering bulbs that also merit a place in the garden.

Situation

A mature bulb contains all that is necessary for the plant to grow and flower. This means that bulbs are an easy and reliable way of producing colour during the first year after they are planted. It also means that they can be used in places where other plants would not survive, because they can 'sit out' a period of drought, darkness or extreme heat or cold. However, they will not tolerate water-logging, and they must have good conditions –

Early-flowering bulbs like snowdrops and winter aconites are valuable for newly-emerged insects

light, moisture and nourishment – during the time they *are* growing, so that the food supply in the bulb can be replenished.

In fact bulbs do not need a rich soil. Peat or leafmould should be dug in to help retain moisture if necessary – imagine the woodland soil to which many bulbs are accustomed. Well-rotted compost can be used on poor soils, but never fresh manure.

The easiest bulbs to grow are those that can be left in the ground to flower and multiply year after year. Vigorous spring-flowering bulbs can be planted in lawns or rough grass (see page 100). You must be prepared to leave the grass uncut for at least six weeks after the flowers have faded, so only the earliest are suitable for lawns. Other spring bulbs will grow under deciduous trees and shrubs, but the combination must be such that the bulbs flower and fade before the canopy of leaves becomes too dense.

In open borders, bulbs must be placed where they will not be disturbed by other planting, but they can be most effective in spring when other flowers are scarce; in summer their dying foliage is hidden by the growth of herbaceous plants. Hardy summer-flowering bulbs such as alliums and autumn-flowering ones such as nerines can also be planted here.

Planting

Nearly all spring-flowering bulbs should be planted in autumn, and autumn-flowering bulbs planted in spring – but there are exceptions, and there is no general rule for summer bulbs. Check on the type before buying; details of a selection of bulbs are given on page 100. Their spacing can be as close as 7.5 cm (3 in) for tiny bulbs like snowdrops, and up to 20 cm (8 in) for large daffodils. They look more natural in groups of one variety, with perhaps a few of the same individual bulbs dotted irregularly outside the main group.

The planting depth depends on the size of bulb and type of soil – the larger the bulb and the lighter the soil, the deeper they should be planted. Too deep and the shoot will be weak when it reaches the surface; too shallow and it could be affected by cold and drought. As a rough guide, the bulb should be covered by a depth of soil three times its height – but again there are exceptions, so it is as well to check.

After-care

It is essential that the leaves are left on the bulb for as long as possible after it has flowered, for this is when they are storing the food for next year's blooms. As already mentioned, grass where bulbs are naturalized should not be cut for at least six weeks after the flowers have faded; in borders the leaves should be left until they wither.

A mulch of well-rotted compost or leafmould in autumn, and a scattering of bonemeal on poor soil, should be all that is necessary to feed the bulbs. However, if after a few years they have multiplied and become crowded so that few large blooms are produced, they should be lifted and the soil replenished. The bulbs and their small offsets can then be replanted over a larger area.

Bulbs can be affected by common soil pests like vine weevil and wireworms, and they also have some specific pests and diseases like the various bulb rots (see page 111) and virus diseases. It is thus most important to buy bulbs from a reliable source. Examine them carefully and discard any that show signs of fungus disease, as these will never give healthy plants and the disease may spread in the soil.

Herbaceous perennials

Herbaceous perennial plants are ones that live for several years (strictly, three or more) but die down in winter. As the majority bloom during the period from June to September, those that have attractive foliage or seedheads, or that keep a low covering of leaves throughout the winter, are the most valuable.

Choose species rather than highly-bred, large-flowered varieties – they will have more pollen and nectar for insects

Situation

Most herbaceous perennials like a reasonably good, well-drained soil; heavy soils should be lightened with leafmould or peat, and poorer soils with well-rotted compost. A sheltered spot is essential for the taller plants, and some of these can be *very* tall – for example, goatsbeard (*Aruncus*) can grow up to 2 m (6 ft). It is advisable to check on the height of plants before you buy. Tall plants should obviously go at the back of a border, but should not be planted right up against a wall or fence, where it can be very dry. A hedge can create similar conditions, but provided that the soil is good there are some low plants that will grow along the bottom: violets, primroses and spotted deadnettle, for example.

RECOMMENDED HERBACEOUS PERENNIALS

Name	Height	Flower type and flowering time	Growing conditions	Comment
BUGLE (*Ajuga reptans*)	10–15 cm (4–6 in)	Blue; May-Aug.	Moist, shady places.	The native species with dark green leaves is best, but there are garden varieties with bronze and variegated leaves. A useful ground cover plant under shrubs.
CATMINT (*Nepeta × faassenii*)	30–45 cm (12–18 in)	Lavender blue; May-Sept.	Any well-drained soil; sunny position.	Attractive grey/green foliage; popular with bees and white butterflies.
CHRISTMAS ROSE (*Helleborus niger*)	30–45 cm (12–18 in)	White with gold stamens; Jan-March.	Moist but well-drained soil; partly shaded position.	Dark evergreen leaves; dislikes disturbance.
ELEPHANT'S EAR (*Bergenia* species)	23–30 cm (9–12 in)	Pink; March-April.	All types of soil; sun or partial shade.	Large leaves form an attractive evergreen mound. Useful early nectar plant for bees and butterflies.
GLOBE THISTLE (*Echinops ritro*)	1–1.2 m (3–4 ft)	Steely blue; July-Sept.	Any well-drained soil; full sun.	A tall, stiff and fairly tidy plant. Flowers loved by bees and butterflies, and seedheads by birds.
GOLDEN ROD (*Solidago* species)	Up to 2 m (6 ft); dwarf hybrids 30–60 cm (1–2 ft) are preferable	Yellow; Aug-Sept.	Any well-drained soil; sun or light shade.	A good late food plant for many insects and has useful seedheads.
ICE PLANT (*Sedum spectabile*)	30–60 cm (1–2 ft)	Pink; Aug-Oct.	Well-drained soil; sunny position; tolerant of dry conditions.	Attractive, grey/green, fleshy leaves form a compact mound. This species (but *not* the hybrids) is one of the best butterfly plants.
LADY'S MANTLE (*Alchemilla mollis*)	30 cm (1 ft)	Greenish yellow; June-Aug.	Any well-drained soil; sun or light shade.	Rounded, light green leaves that catch the dew make the plant attractive when not in flower.
LUNGWORT (*Pulmonaria* species)	30 cm (1 ft)	Blue/pink mixed; April-May.	Moist soil with plenty of organic matter; light shade.	Some species have attractive silver markings on leaves.
MEADOW CRANESBILL (*Geranium pratense*)	45 cm (18 in)	Deep blue; June-Aug.	Any ordinary soil; sun or light shade.	This is the native species but there are garden varieties that are also good bee plants. Attractive seedheads for birds.

Planting

The best time for planting bare-rooted plants is early spring, but it can be done in autumn or during mild spells in winter. Plants in containers can be set out at any time, but need watering well in summer.

They look best in clumps, ideally using three to five plants of one type spaced so that there is no bare earth visible between them in summer. The distance can be anything from 15 cm (6 in) to 60 cm (2 ft), depending on the height and spread of the plant, and is usually best judged by experience. Most herbaceous plants needs regular lifting and splitting (see below), so any that have become swamped can be rescued at that time.

RECOMMENDED HERBACEOUS PERENNIALS (cont.)

Name	Height	Flower type and flowering time	Growing conditions	Comment
MICHAELMAS DAISY (*Aster* species)	Up to 1.2 m (4 ft) but dwarf varieties 30 cm (12 in) preferable	Purple/blue/pink; Aug-Oct.	Rich, moist soils; sunny position.	Useful for late colour and for bees and butterflies. Mildew can be a problem (see page 111).
PASQUE FLOWER (*Pulsatilla vulgaris*)	30 cm (12 in)	Purple with gold stamens; April-May.	A well-drained soil; sunny position.	A beautiful native downland plant; attractive fluffy seedheads. Can be difficult to establish and dislikes disturbance.
PRIMROSE (*Primula vulgaris*)	15 cm (6 in)	Yellow; March-May.	Reasonably fertile, moist soil; position that is shady in summer.	This is the native species but the colourful garden varieties and the hybrid polyanthus are also useful spring flowers.
SHASTA DAISY (*Chrysanthemum maximum*)	60–90 cm (2–3 ft)	White with yellow centres; June-Aug.	Fairly fertile, well-drained soil; sunny position.	Flat, open flowers good for hoverflies.
SOAPWORT (*Saponaria officinalis*)	60–90 cm (2–3 ft)	Pink; Aug-Sept; slightly scented.	Any well-drained soil; sun or light shade.	Often found naturalized in the wild – can be invasive; attracts hawk moths.
SPOTTED DEADNETTLE (*Lamium maculatum*)	30 cm (12 in)	Pink/purple; May-July.	Any soil; shady position.	Useful ground cover – clip off old growth after flowering. A good bee plant.
VALERIAN (*Centranthus ruber*)	60 cm (2 ft)	Deep pink; June-Sept.	Any well-drained soil (often grows out of walls); sunny position.	One of the best flowers for attracting bees and butterflies.
VIOLET (*Viola odorata*)	10–15 cm (4–6 in)	Blue or white; Feb-April and sometimes in autumn; sweet scent.	Moist but well-drained soil; light shade.	A native flower that will grow under deciduous shrubs or trees.
YARROW (*Achillea* species)	60–90 cm (2–3 ft)	Pink/red/yellow; June-Sept.	Ordinary well-drained soil; sunny position; will tolerate dry conditions.	*A. millefolium* is the wild species of which there are garden varieties, but all the yarrows with flat flowerheads are good for bees, butterflies and hoverflies.

After-care

A late spring mulch of compost should be all that is needed to feed the plants, and it will also help to keep the ground weed free until their leaves grow up and cover it. Removing faded blooms from some early summer flowers can encourage a second burst of colour, but later remember to leave some seedheads for the birds. Dead foliage should be removed in autumn if there are any signs of disease, but otherwise could be left until early spring.

The best way to keep most herbaceous plants healthy is to lift each clump every three or four years, and discard the old centre. More compost or leafmould can then be dug into the soil, and the young, vigorous parts from the outside of the clump replanted. There are, however, a number of plants that do better if left undisturbed: hellebores and Japanese anemones are two common examples.

There are few pests and diseases that vigorously growing herbaceous plants cannot overcome, though some will show symptoms (see page 111).

Roses

There are types of rose suitable for almost any garden – large or small, formal or informal. Many of them have no need of the chemical fertilizers, pesticides and fungicides sold especially for roses in garden shops.

Those roses that the catalogues call **large flowered** and **cluster flowered bush roses** are the modern rose-bed roses (the hybrid teas and floribundas). They flower continuously from mid summer until the autumn frosts, and many of the newest varieties have been bred to have both disease resistance and scent. Against this, however, they need good soil conditions to flourish, and their formal appearance makes them uncomfortable partners for many of the loose and flowery 'cottage garden' plants. On their own they are exceedingly dull during the seven or eight months

that they are not in flower, and the closely folded blooms that look so perfect in the drawing-room rose bowl are no use to bees or other nectar-seeking insects. The larger modern shrub roses have similar properties.

There are many hundreds of modern rose varieties, and more are introduced each year, so it is difficult to make recommendations; however, those on page 108 have established a reputation for good disease resistance, vigour and, where possible, scent.

Only a few of the **old garden roses**, like the 'China', 'Alba' and 'Damask' shrub roses, are still available. They have the soft colours, sweet scent and lax growth associated with gardens of the past, but many are large and suffer badly from blackspot and mildew – though there are exceptions (see page 111).

It is the **wild** or **species roses** that have most to offer. A few are native to Britain, but more grow wild in China and Japan and other parts of the

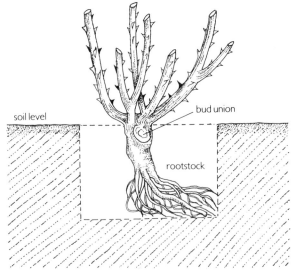

Planting a modern bush rose
Prepare a planting hole large enough to accommodate the roots. Then, holding the rose in position, fill in with good soil mixed with compost firming as you go. Make sure the bud union is below soil level

world. They have simple flowers, producing plenty of pollen, which are usually followed by large red hips. These fruit and the attractive foliage more than make up for their often short flowering period. Although the true species are often vigorous sprawling bushes, there are a few cultivated forms suitable even for small gardens. They fit well into mixed borders and some can also be planted in hedges or rough grass.

Climbing roses should be chosen with great care. Some can climb up to 7.6 m (25 ft) and are extremely difficult to restrain! The ramblers make the most vigorous growth, producing many long new shoots each year. They are better grown over arches and up pillars than against walls, where the dry conditions make them increasingly susceptible to mildew. The modern climbers, which bear flowers on a more or less permanent framework of stems, are far more suited to this position.

Situation

The essential condition for all types of rose is good drainage. Waterlogged ground apart, there are some roses that will grow in most positions. Modern bush, shrub and climbing roses need a deep, rich soil; plenty of compost or well-rotted manure must be dug into light or shallow ones. However, some of the wild roses, like varieties of *R.rugosa*, and a few of the old garden roses do well in poor soils. A sunny position is desirable for nearly all roses, and particularly necessary for the modern bushes and shrubs. However, some climbers will grow on a north or east wall provided that it is in a fairly open position and there is plenty of indirect light.

Planting

Bare-rooted plants can be put in any time between November and March, the earlier the better. Modern bush roses should be spaced about 60 cm (2 ft) apart, and climbers and ramblers at least 2.1 m (7 ft); the spacing of any of the shrub roses depends on their size – they usually need about 1.2–2.5 m (4–8 ft).

Roses and the perennial lady's mantle (*Alchemilla mollis*)

Most roses are not grown on their own roots but are 'budded' onto rootstocks. The bushes should be planted so that the 'bud union' is about 2.5 cm (1 in) below the soil surface.

After-care

All types of rose benefit from an annual mulch of well-rotted manure or compost and, on poor soils, a sprinkling of bonemeal. Cut off the fading blooms of the modern perpetual-flowering varieties (but *not* of the wild roses, where attractive hips will form).

The principles behind rose pruning are very similar to those of fruit pruning (see page 72). All types of shrub rose need little more than the removal of dead and congested wood; if old stems start to become bare at the base, then one or two can be cut right back to induce new growth. Modern bush roses, climbers and ramblers need more careful pruning. Ramblers should be pruned in late summer or autumn, when flowering has finished. Other types of roses are best pruned in the spring (mid-March to early April) just as growth is beginning.

From the many pests and diseases listed in rose books, it may seem surprising that they can be grown organically at all. However, most of the pests occur in very small numbers and can be picked off by hand when the damage is first spotted, though greenfly can be a problem; similarly the main diseases – blackspot and mildew – can be avoided by choice of variety and good growing conditions (see page 111).

RECOMMENDED ROSE VARIETIES

Variety	Type	Height	Flowers	Flowering period
ALEC'S RED	Large flowered	1 m (3 ft)	Crimson, very fragrant	Repeat flowering
KING'S RANSOM	Large flowered	75 cm (2½ ft)	Yellow, fragrant	Repeat flowering
SILVER JUBILEE	Large flowered	75 cm (2½ ft)	Coral pink, fragrant	Repeat flowering
ARTHUR BELL	Cluster flowered	1.1 m (3½ ft)	Yellow, very fragrant	Repeat flowering
ESCAPADE	Cluster flowered	75 cm (2½ ft)	Magenta, musky scent	Repeat flowering
MARGARET MERRIL	Cluster flowered	1 m (3 ft)	White, very fragrant	Repeat flowering
SCENTED AIR	Cluster flowered	1 m (3 ft)	Deep pink, very fragrant	Repeat flowering
FRED LOADS	Modern shrub	1.8 m (6 ft)	Vermillion, single, fragrant	Repeat flowering
GOLDEN WINGS	Modern shrub	1.8 m (6 ft)	Yellow, single, fragrant	Repeat flowering
PERLE D'OR	Old garden (China)	1.2 m (4 ft)	Apricot, double, slightly fragrant	Repeat flowering
QUEEN OF DENMARK	Old garden (Alba)	1.5 m (5 ft)	Pink, double, very fragrant	Late June/July
R. RUBIFOLIA	Wild	1.5 m (5 ft)	Pink, small, single, followed by red hips; foliage dusky purple	June
R. RUGOSA (Frau Dagmar Hartopp)	Wild	1.4 m (4½ ft)	Pink, small, single, very fragrant, followed by large hips	June and then intermittently until autumn
R. SPINOSISSIMA (Stanwell Perpetual)	Wild	1.2 m (4 ft)	Light pink, semi-double, fragrant	May-June
ALTISSIMO	Climber	2.5 m (8 ft)	Red, large, single, slightly fragrant	Repeat flowering
SCHOOLGIRL	Climber	3 m (10 ft)	Dusky orange, large flowered type, fragrant	Repeat flowering
ALOHA	Climber	2.5 m (8 ft)	Deep pink, large flowered type, fragrant	Repeat flowering
WHITE COCKADE	Climber	2.3 m (7 ft)	White, double, slightly fragrant	Repeat flowering

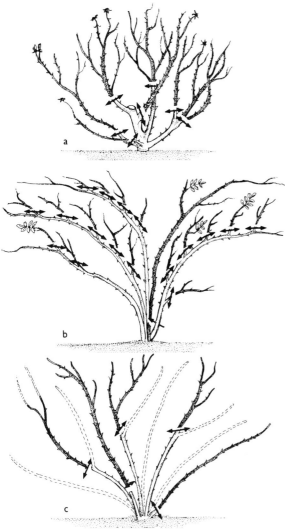

Shrubs and climbers

Shrubs have a framework of woody stems rising from ground level; they can be anything up to several metres in height, although there are many suitable for small gardens. Some can be trained against a wall or fence, either woven through a trellis or tied onto wires. True climbers are those that have special clinging or twining mechanisms – like the roots of ivy or the tendrils of vines.

Situation

There are shrubs and climbers that will match almost any growing conditions, even water-logged soils or heavy shade. However, a wider range can be grown if the soil conditions are improved by adding peat or leafmould to heavy soils, and compost or well-rotted manure to poor ones. A few shrubs have specific likes and dislikes – some need an acid soil, for example – so check this before making a choice. Also check their final size – keeping a large, vigorous shrub under control in a small garden can be a constant battle and destroy much of its beauty.

Planting

Bare-rooted deciduous shrubs should be planted when they are dormant – from mid-October to mid-March – whenever weather conditions are suitable. Deciduous shrubs and climbers in pots can be planted throughout the year provided that they are watered well. Evergreens should not be planted during the winter months because they lose water through their leaves that cannot be replaced if the ground is frozen. They are best planted in early autumn or late spring, though container grown ones can be planted in summer.

The spacing depends on the mature height and spread of the shrub, and the latter is not always easy to determine. If no other guidelines are available, space any two shrubs at a distance of half the sum of their heights – for example, a 2 m (6 ft) shrub and a 1.2 m (4 ft) shrub should be spaced

(a) Pruning a modern bush rose Cut out any diseased or broken stems, crossing branches and spindly shoots. Cut vigorous shoot back to five to seven buds on the old wood, and weak ones to about three
(b) Pruning climbers Climbers bear flowers on short side shoots on a semi-permanent framework of branches. Cut each side shoot back to two or three buds. Train framework branches at an angle to encourage the formation of side shoots and flowers. Cut out old framework branches that have become bare at the base to encourage new growth
(c) Pruning ramblers Ramblers bear most flowers on new growth produced the previous summer. Cut out old stems that have flowered down to ground level where there is new growth to replace them (1) or back to the point where the new growth has begun (2)

1.6 m (5 ft) apart. They should always be planted at the same depth as they were in the nursery. Unless the soil is very good, fill in the planting hole with a mixture of soil and peat (or leafmould) and add bonemeal (about 50 g (2 oz) per bucketful of mixture).

After-care

Mulch the base of shrubs and climbers in late spring; leafmould, forest bark or woodchips (see page 19) are the most suitable materials. Those planted in grass should have an area of at least 1 m (3 ft) diameter cleared around them. They may need to be watered during dry spells for the first year or two, but once they are established most need little watering or feeding. Extra nutrients – in the form of a compost mulch and/or bonemeal – are most needed for shrubs that are pruned hard and have to make a lot of new growth each year.

Pruning shrubs is usually a lot less complicated than pruning fruit trees, but it is always wise to check the specific method for pruning any shrub that you buy. The initial aims are always the same: to remove any dead and diseased wood, to cut out weak or overcrowded branches and to keep the shrub in shape. Many need little more than this, though there are exceptions.

It is, however, essential to prune at the right time, and this also varies from species to species. In general, spring-flowering shrubs should be pruned as soon as they have finished flowering because the growth the shrub makes that summer will bear next year's flowers. Summer-flowering shrubs are usually pruned in late winter because the shoots that grow in spring bear the flowers. Evergreens are usually pruned in early summer so that any subsequent growth has time to harden before the winter.

Established shrubs rarely suffer from any disabling pest or disease attacks, and troubles with new ones are much more likely to be caused by the wrong soil or weather conditions. Most of those that do occur are shared with other ornamental plants or fruit trees – caterpillars, leafminer aphids, powdery mildew, rust, die back and coral spot, for example; they should be readily recognizable and similarly treated.

One disease that can cause fatal damage is the infamous honey fungus. It grows quite happily on dead wood, but can send out long, tough, black underground threads and infect living trees and shrubs through their roots. The associated golden yellow toadstools appear in autumn. The result can be devastating. However, vigorous, healthy shrubs are not usually affected, and it is possible that in the balanced environment of the organic garden the effects of this harmful fungus are counteracted by beneficial ones. It has been suggested that *Trichoderma* (see page 36) might help to control honey fungus, so it would be worth trying on infected trees.

After all the hard work it is important to have a pleasant spot to relax and to reflect in the organic garden

COMMON PESTS AND DISEASES OF ORNAMENTAL PLANTS

PEST	Symptom	Plants susceptible	Avoidance/control
APHIDS	Affect young leaves and shoots; plant becomes sticky with honeydew.	Any; particularly blackfly on nasturtiums, viburnums and honeysuckle, and greenfly on roses.	Pick off infected shoots of nasturtiums when first seen. Spray with insecticidal soap or derris (page 36).
CHAFERS	Holes in leaves and sometimes flowers. Larvae in soil feed on roots and bulbs.	Any; damage by rose chafer commonly seen on roses.	Control adult chafer by hand picking – damage is seldom severe. Forking round plants helps to reduce numbers of larvae.
EELWORM	Distorted, yellowing and wilting leaves. Bulbs that are affected show brown rings if they are cut open.	Bulbs – narcissi, hyacinth, snowdrop, tulip. Herbaceous plants – phlox and primulas.	Destroy infected plants and do not replant susceptible varieties on the same spot for at least three years.
FLEABEETLE	Small round holes in seedling leaves, particularly in hot, dry weather.	Plants of the brassica family like alyssum and wallflowers.	Keep seedlings growing strongly. Dust or spray with derris.
LEAFHOPPER	Mottled leaves.	Roses.	Damage not often serious on mature plants. Spray as for aphids if necessary.
LEAFMINER	Tunnels visible in leaves.	Any, particularly shasta daisies.	Pick off and destroy affected leaves.
NARCISSUS FLY	Soft bulbs; stunted leaves; no flowers.	Daffodils and other narcissi, snowdrops, snowflakes.	Destroy soft bulbs; fill in holes left by dying leaves to prevent the fly from laying its eggs.
SWIFT MOTH	Tissue of rhizomes eaten away by larvae.	Irises, lily-of-the-valley.	Keep ground around the plants well weeded and forked.
DISEASE			
BLACKSPOT	Round black spots with fringed edges on leaves.	Roses.	Avoid planting in close conditions. Clear away fallen leaves. Use resistant varieties.
BULB ROTS (see also tulip fire, white rot)	Yellow, stunted shoots; soft bulbs.	Any.	Do not plant soft bulbs or plant in badly drained soil. Dig up and destroy infected plants. Use less susceptible varieties.
BOTRYTIS	Grey mould on leaves, stems and flowers.	Any, but common on bedding plants like petunias.	Avoid damp and crowded conditions. Pick off infected parts of plants.
CLUB ROOT	Swollen roots; plants stunted.	Plants in brassica family.	Lime acid soils. Do not replant susceptible varieties on infected soil.
DIE BACK	The ends of stems become unhealthy and die.	Very common on roses.	Cut infected shoots back to live tissue. Avoid waterlogged conditions. Can also be caused by root damage or frost.
DRY ROT	Corms go hard and shrivel.	Crocus.	Inspect bulbs before planting. Destroy diseased plants.
LEAF SPOT	Dark blotches or rings on leaves.	Many herbaceous plants and shrubs, e.g. hellebores, willows.	Remove and destroy infected leaves when they are first seen; clear debris in autumn.
POWDERY MILDEW	White coating on leaves and stems.	Many annuals, herbaceous plants and roses, particularly forget-me-nots, Michaelmas daisies, delphiniums, golden rod and phlox.	Avoid dry, overcrowded conditions. Water and mulch plants. Divide herbaceous plants regularly. Use resistant varieties of roses; aster species like *A. amellus* are less prone than the true Michaelmas daisies.
RUST	Orange/brown spots on leaves and stems.	Many including sweet williams, hollyhocks, antirrhinums, bluebells, carnations, roses, berberis.	Worse in poor conditions. Remove diseased material as soon as possible. Use rust-resistant antirrhinum varieties.
TULIP FIRE	Scorched areas on leaves, spots on flowers; bulbs rot.	Tulips.	Do not plant soft bulbs or plant in cold, wet places. Destroy infected plants.
VIRUS DISEASES	Symptoms include mottled and distorted leaves and flowers, stunted growth or loss of vigour.	Any; tulips and lilies are often very susceptible.	Dig up and destroy affected plants. Buy plants and bulbs from a reputable source.
WHITE ROT	Fluffy white growth on bulbs.	Alliums.	Dig up and destroy infected plants. Do not replant ornamental alliums (or any onions or garlic) in this spot.

RECOMMENDED SHRUBS AND CLIMBERS

SHRUBS	Height	Description
BERBERIS THUNBERGII	1.5 m (5 ft)	Pale yellow scented flowers in April/May; light green leaves turning red in autumn; red berries.
BUDDLEIA DAVIDII	2.5 m (8 ft) but can be restricted by pruning.	Mauve flowers; July-Sept; deciduous. The most popular butterfly shrub.
COTONEASTER HORIZONTALIS	60 cm (2 ft) if allowed to spread, but can be trained against a wall.	Pink and white flowers in June; usually evergreen; red berries.
CHAENOMELES SPECIOSA (Japanese quince)	1.2–2 m (4–6 ft), can be trained against a wall.	Red flowers; March-May; deciduous. Yellow, quince-like fruit in autumn.
CORNUS ALBA (dogwood)	1.5 m (5 ft) if pruned hard	Creamy white flowers in June/July; deciduous. Black berries in autumn; attractive red stems in winter.
CORYLUS AVELLANA (hazel)	3–5 m (9–15 ft) but can be restricted by pruning	Yellow catkins in spring; deciduous. Nuts in autumn. A native shrub.
DAPHNE MEZEREUM	1.5 m (5 ft)	Dark pink, scented flowers in Feb/March; deciduous. Scarlet berries in autumn. A rare native shrub.
HEBE BRACHYSIPHON	2 m (6 ft)	White flowers in June/July; evergreen. Hebes are among the best butterfly shrubs.
ILEX AQUIFOLIUM (holly)	Often 10 m (30 ft) in the wild but slow growing and can be restricted to any size by pruning.	Insignificant white flowers; attractive evergreen leaves; berries if both male and female bushes are planted – or chose a self-fertile garden variety.
MAHONIA AQUIFOLIUM	1–1.5 m (3–5 ft)	Yellow scented flowers in March/April; evergreen. Blue-black berries in autumn.
PYRACANTHA COCCINES	4 m (12 ft) but can be wall-trained and restricted.	Small white flowers in June; evergreen. Red berries in autumn.
SKIMMIA REEVESIANA	1 m (3 ft)	Creamy white scented flowers in June/July; evergreen. Red berries in early autumn.
SYMPHORICARPOS ALBUS (snowberry)	1.5-2 m (5–6 ft)	Small pink flowers June-Aug; deciduous. White berries in autumn.
SYRINGA MICROPHYLLA	1.2–1.5 m (4–5 ft)	Lilac-coloured, scented flowers May/June and often Sept.
VIBURNUM OPULUS Compactum	1.8 m (6 ft)	White scented flowers May/June; deciduous; red berries in autumn. A compact form of the native species.
CLIMBERS		
CLEMATIS TANGUTICA	5–7 m (15–20 ft), but can be restricted; climbs by twining.	Yellow, Aug-Sept; followed by silver seedheads; deciduous.
HEDERA HELIX (ivy)	Depends on variety – native species grows to 20 m (60 ft) or more, but can easily be restricted; clings by aerial roots.	Cream/green flowers Sept-Nov; evergreen; black berries in late winter. Very useful food plant for insects and birds when little else is available. Cultivated forms have attractive leaves – but check that they cling and bear berries.
LONICERA PERICLYMENUM (honeysuckle)	7 m (20 ft), but can be restricted. Climbs by twining.	Reddish purple/yellow scented flowers June-Aug, followed by red berries; deciduous.
HYDRANGEA PETIOLARIS	Up to 20 m (60 ft), but slow growing and can be restricted. Self-clinging.	Large white flowers in June.
VITIS VINIFERA (Brandt)	7 m (20 ft), but can be restricted. Climbs with tendrils.	Green-white flowers in May/June followed by small purple grapes; leaves coloured in autumn; deciduous.

Growing conditions	Pruning
Any reasonable soil; sun or partial shade.	None necessary except tidying.
Any well-drained soil, particularly chalk; sunny position.	Best if pruned hard in March, cutting back last year's growth to within 5 cm (2 in) of old wood.
Any ordinary soil – tolerant of poor conditions; best in sun.	None except when wall-training; remove unwanted branches in spring.
Any reasonable soil; sun or shade.	None for bushes; trim wall-trained shrubs in summer.
Most reasonable soils – will tolerate damp conditions; sun or partial shade.	Cut some stems back to a few inches above ground level in early spring to stimulate new, attractive red growth.
Any well-drained soil; sun or partial shade. Could be planted in a hedge.	Some old branches can be cut to a few inches above the ground in March; this restricts size and gives new growth.
Soil containing plenty of organic matter; sun or partial shade.	None; remove damaged branches after flowering.
Any reasonable well-drained soil; sun or light shade; shelter from cold winds.	Not usually necessary; cut back any leggy bare branches in April.
Best in soil with plenty of organic matter; sun or shade.	Trim in spring to restrict growth.
Any reasonable soil; sun or shade.	Usually none, but cut out untidy growth in April.
Any reasonable soil; sun or partial shade.	Cut back unwanted shoots after flowering.
Any reasonable soil that is not limy; partial shade preferable.	Usually none; remove damaged branches in spring.
Any reasonable soil; sun or shade.	Thin out and cut back unwanted growth in winter, and remove suckers, or the shrub can become invasive. Non-suckering varieties are available.
Any reasonable soil; sunny position.	Immediately after flowering prune back all flowering shoots to the first leaves below the flower cluster. Thin out unwanted branches in winter.
Fairly fertile, moist soil; sunny position.	Usually none, thin out unwanted or damaged branches after flowering.
Fertile, moist soil, preferably alkaline; sunny position though the base of the plant should be in shade.	In spring remove all previous season's stems to within a few inches of the old growth.
Any reasonable soil; sun or shade.	Check by cutting back unwanted growth in spring.
Any ordinary moist but well-drained soil; best in partial shade.	Thin out old or unwanted stems after flowering.
Any ordinary well-drained soil, sun or shade.	Not usually necessary; remove unwanted stems in winter.
Fertile, moist but well-drained soil, preferably alkaline. Sunny position.	In late summer thin out old growth and shorten new growth where necessary.

5
HERBS

A herb can be defined as a plant with powerful natural properties. Some are common ornamental plants; others are to be found growing wild. A few, like parsley, are often grown on a vegetable plot, though they are only used in small quantities by comparison with the crops.

It is not only the leaves of herbs that are harvested but sometimes the seeds, roots, flowers or stems. Their properties make them useful in both house and garden. They are reputed to benefit crops and also to deter pests, and they attract butterflies, bees and other beneficial insects. They can replace artificial products in cooking and various other household tasks, and provide a safe remedy for many minor ailments.

The uses to which individual herbs are put are determined by the 'active' substances they contain. The pungent smell and taste of familiar culinary herbs like sage and thyme come from aromatic oils. These oils are very volatile, and their presence influences how the herbs should be grown, harvested and preserved. The same oils also have medicinal properties, ranging from being gentle aids to digestion to being strongly antiseptic.

Less obvious are the wide range of vitamins and minerals in fresh herbs: parsley leaves, for example, contain significant amounts of iron, calcium, phosphorus and manganese, and vitamins C and A. Herbs are thus a healthy addition to

Opposite: Traditionally herbs have been grown in sheltered beds edged with a low-box hedge. Other patterns are shown on page 117

our diet and similarly make a valuable contribution to the compost heap.

The other constituents of herbs are mainly made use of in herbal remedies – substances that are bitter, astringent or mucilaganeous. Most of these are safe to use at home, though of course it is essential to identify the herb correctly. A few contain very poisonous substances but are nevertheless useful to qualified herbalists: foxgloves and deadly nightshade are two examples.

Herbs around the garden

To decide where to plant a herb, it is necessary to know the conditions it needs, whether it is annual or perennial, its height and what parts of the plant are to be used.

Herbs vary widely in their requirements, and these are sometimes surprising. It often helps to find out where the plants grow in the wild. Only if they are grown in similar conditions in the garden will they reach their full potential.

Many of the shrubby, dry-leaved herbs such as rosemary, thyme, lavender, sage and winter savory are native to the rocky hillsides of the Mediterranéan, and all need sunshine and a light, well-drained soil to do well. A rich soil or moist, shady conditions will cause lush growth in which the aromatic oils lose their strength; chemical fertilizers have an equally weakening effect.

Many herbaceous herbs like fennel, tarragon, lovage and salad burnet similarly need sunshine and good drainage, as do the annuals dill, fennel and basil, though all these do well in slightly richer soils.

In preparing the ground for these herbs, it is important to fork deeply to remove any compaction. Work peat or leafmould into heavy soils. Well-rotted compost can be used on light soils, but never fresh manure. On very heavy soils or those prone to waterlogging, a raised herb bed may be the answer. This can be no more than 30 cm (12 in) or so high – made as described in Chapter 1 – or one contained by a proper wall up to about 60 cm (2 ft) high.

Not all herbs need such sunny, dry conditions, however. Mints, for example, generally grow wild in watery places and therefore flourish in a rich, moisture-retentive soil. Often they then grow *too* well, the roots creeping among the roots of other plants and up between paving stones! They are best contained using buckets, heavy gauge polythene bags or other containers sunk into the ground. Make drainage holes in the bottom of the container, fill it with soil and compost so that no part of it shows, and plant the mint inside. Parsley, chives, sweet cicely, comfrey, horseradish and angelica need similar moist soils, and all these herbs flourish in partial shade.

Shelter from the wind is almost as important as sunshine for some of the more tender species – basil and rosemary, for example – and it can be equally desirable for tall, flimsy herbs that otherwise would need staking. Ideally, all the aromatic herbs should be grown in sheltered spots where their warm scents and flowers can be best appreciated. The insects, too, like the shelter. Herbs in the Umbelliferae and Compositae families, with their open flowerheads, attract the hoverflies, while those in the Labiatae are most visited by bees.

Herbs need not necessarily be confined to a herb garden; they can be mixed with flowers, fruit, shrubs and even vegetables. In this way, they can be given the individual conditions they need and at the same time benefit other plants. Herbs are often said to be good 'companions', directly enhancing the growth of other plants, but there is little evidence that this is true. However, the scent of the herbs and the mixture of different plants may help to deceive pests, and the herb flowers encourage bees and hoverflies as well as looking attractive.

Some medicinal herbs will usually be in the garden already as they are common garden 'weeds'! These need only to be left to flourish in appropriate places. Yarrow, dandelion and ribwort plantain, for example, are common in lawns, and allowing the grass to grow long in some out of the way corner will give supplies for picking. Chickweed will inevitably appear on a manured vegetable patch throughout the year, and some can be left where it will not harm the crop. Brambles and elder can form part of an informal hedge, and this is also a place where hops and goosegrass can scramble.

Left: Herbs in the botanical family Labiatae have flowers with a lip on which bees can alight when visiting them for nectar. Such herbs include lemon balm, mint, rosemary, basil, thyme, marjoram, lavender, sage and savory

Right: Those in the family Umbelliferae have a flat open umbel of flowers which give easy access to hoverflies. Such herbs include dill, fennel, chervil, caraway, parsley, angelica, lovage and sweet cicely

It is the annual and biennial herbs like parsley, dill, chervil, garlic, pot marigolds and rocket that are the most appropriate to grow on vegetable beds, as these can be made to fit in with the sowing and harvesting dates and rotation of the crops. For example, garlic – in the *Allium* family – obviously fits on the onion bed, whereas chervil, which is most useful in autumn and early spring, goes well with an overwintering crop like spinach beet. Long-growing perennials can conveniently be used as edgings to vegetable beds, especially those that are used in large quantities like chives and salad burnet.

An odd corner of the vegetable garden is one of the best places for herbs like horseradish, which are grown for their roots. Here digging them up for harvest does not disturb other plants.

Herbs grown among fruit must not interfere with mulching or picking the crop. Low-growing, shade-loving plants like woodruff could be grown in the deep soil among currant or gooseberry bushes, and low, bushy herbs like thyme, lavender and marjoram in the sun round wall-trained trees.

Nearly all the shrubby herbs make attractive additions to an ornamental border: some, like lavender and hyssop, for their lasting flowers; others for their foliage, as they generally keep their leaves throughout the winter. The silver and grey-leaved shrubs, like rosemary and santolina and the variegated forms of thyme and sage, are particularly effective. Bear in mind, however, that the cultivated forms are sometimes not as good for cooking or medicine as the native species.

There are also herbaceous herbs with attractive flowers and foliage: bergamot, with its colourful red blooms, and fennel, with its delicate feathery foliage, are both ideal in a flowerbed. Low-growing, shade-loving herbs like woodruff and periwinkle are best among shrubs, while the sun-loving creeping thymes can fill gaps between paving stones.

The size of a herb obviously influences where it can be planted, but remember that many benefit from being kept cut back. This produces the fresh young growth which is best for cooking and other

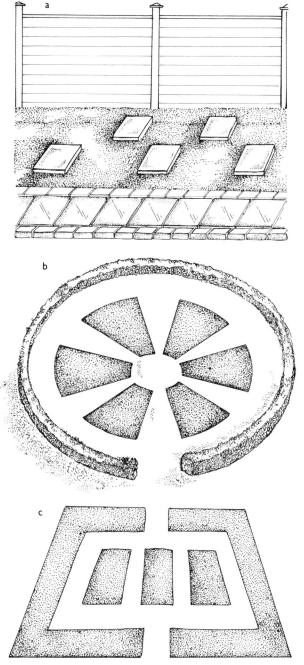

Simple designs for a herb bed that give easy access to every plant (a) A narrow border with stepping stones (b) A wheel with paths along the spokes (c) A nest of rectangles

uses. Tall herbs like fennel and lovage can be grown even in a small garden if kept clipped to about 30 cm (12 in) above the ground. To harvest seeds, however, the plants must be left to flower and reach their full height of 1.2 m (4 ft) or more.

Herbs can thus be grown throughout the garden, but it is still useful to have your favourites near to hand. This might mean a special bed near the kitchen door or, in a small garden, perhaps just a few pots on the patio. Here they can conveniently be picked for cooking – and you can sit out and enjoy their fragrance and flowers!

Ideally you should be able to reach every herb from a path. A narrow border about two plants deep would allow this, as would a wider one with stepping stones. There is also scope for more intricate designs; a wheel with paths along the spokes, a spiral, or a nest of rectangles, for example.

Many herbs grow extremely well in pots. The shrubby aromatic herbs can tolerate the sometimes hot and dry conditions, and keep their shape well if regularly clipped. Softer herbaceous and annual herbs such as parsley, chives and basil can also be successful – but they must be kept watered, fed and picked to encourage young leaves to grow. They can be planted in a cluster of individual 15–20 cm (6–8 in) pots or in a trough, half-barrel or other large container.

Sowing and planting

Hardy annual herbs like dill, borage, rocket and chervil are best sown directly in the garden – in rows like vegetable seeds or in patches (see page 20). Most germinate readily and they will re-sow themselves, giving a succession of plants for harvesting. This can sometimes be a disadvantage, however: borage seedlings, for example, may need to be weeded out from all parts of the garden. Biennials like parsley and mullein are often sown directly, but they will transplant readily and so can be started off in pots or trays indoors. This is the best way of dealing with seeds that are small or

HERBS FOR THE GARDEN

Name	Type	Height
ANGELICA	Perennial (short-lived)	2 m (6 ft)
BASIL	Half-hardy annual	30–60 cm (1–2 ft)
BAY	Slow-growing tree, evergreen	5.5 m (18 ft)
BERGAMOT	Hardy herbaceous perennial	60 cm (2 ft)
BORAGE	Annual	45–75 cm (1½–2½ ft)
CHAMOMILE (Roman)	Hardy perennial	30 cm (1 ft)
CHERVIL	Annual	30–60 cm (1–2 ft)
CHIVES	Herbaceous perennial	20 cm (8 in)
COMFREY (wild)	Herbaceous perennial (native)	1 m (3 ft)
DILL	Annual	75 cm (2½ ft)
FENNEL	Hardy herbaceous perennial	1.5 m (5 ft)
GARLIC	Grown as a hardy annual	45 cm (1½ ft)
HORSERADISH	Hardy herbaceous perennial	60 cm (2 ft)
HYSSOP	Hardy shrub, evergreen in mild winters	45 cm (1½ ft)
LAVENDER	Hardy evergreen shrub	30 cm–1 m (1–3 ft) depending on variety.
LEMON BALM	Hardy herbaceous perennial	60 cm–1 m (2–3 ft)

Growing position	Method of growing	Uses
Rich soil, partial shade. Attractive in a large flower border.	From seed, which must be fresh, but readily self-seeds.	Leaves and stalks mainly used in sweet cookery. Difficult to dry. Flowerheads attract hoverflies.
Rich, well-drained soil. Warm, sheltered position or grow in pots in a greenhouse. Foliage attractive if growing well, especially the purple form.	From seed sown in heat.	Leaves have a distinctive flavour – much used in cooking and sometimes medicinally. Difficult to dry.
Warm, sheltered position, or grow in pots which can be taken indoors in winter.	Best to buy plants.	A traditional culinary herb. Dries well.
Rich, moist soil, partial shade. Colourful red or pink flowers make it an attractive border plant.	By seed except for named varieties; plants can be divided.	Makes a delicious herb tea. Some medicinal value. Dries fairly well.
Any soil, sunny position. Attractive flowers but sprawling growth – best in a large flower bed or an unused corner.	From seed; readily self-seeds.	Flowers used for decoration, fresh in salad or drinks, dried in pot-pourri. A very good bee plant.
Any soil, sunny position, good ground cover, particularly the low, non-flowering 'Treneague' variety.	Seed or offsets from established plants.	Flowers used as a herb tea; also used medicinally. Dries well.
Fairly moist soil, partial shade in summer.	Seed sown outside – early spring or late summer (self-seeds readily).	Used fresh in salad and cooking – can be picked in winter if put under cloches. Does not dry well.
Rich, moist soil; sunny position. Edging herb.	Seed or division of clumps.	Leaves used fresh in cooking and salad. Does not dry well. Flowers attract bees.
Rich, damp soil; sun or partial shade.	Divide plants: will grow from pieces of root.	A valuable healing herb – roots and leaves used. Various garden uses (see page 25).
Well-drained soil, sunny position.	Seed sown outside in April.	A traditional culinary and medicinal herb – leaves, flowerheads and seed used. Does not dry well. Flowerheads attract hoverflies.
Well-drained, fairly rich soil; sunny position. Foliage attractive in flower beds, especially the bronze form.	From seed sown outside in spring (self-seeds readily) or by division of clumps.	A traditional culinary herb – mainly leaves used. Also of medicinal value. Does not dry well. Flowerheads attract hoverflies.
Well-drained but rich soil; sunny position.	From cloves planted in late autumn or early spring.	Well-known culinary herb, but also of great medicinal value.
Deep, light, well-manured soil. Best in a permanent patch of its own – easily spreads.	Will grow from pieces of root.	Traditional culinary herb, also with medicinal uses.
Well-drained soil; sunny position. Used for hedges and in flower border.	From seed sown in pots indoors.	A pungent herb which was once used in cooking and medicine. Most useful for its attractive flowers, loved by bees and butterflies.
Well-drained soil; sunny position. Good for hedges and flower borders.	Some varieties from seed sown in pots indoors in spring; others, take cuttings or buy plants.	Dried flowers traditionally used in pot-pourri. A good bee and butterfly plant.
Fairly rich, moist soil; sunny position. Not a particularly attractive plant, though there is a variegated form.	From seed (self-seeds readily), or can divide clumps.	Fresh leaves make a pleasant herb tea; some medicinal uses. Does not dry well. One of the best bee plants.

slow to germinate. Sowings can be made in spring and sometimes also in autumn (see pages 118–21).

The few half-hardy annuals like basil and sweet marjoram must be started off in early spring in pots in the warm. They can be transplanted to sunny, sheltered spots in the garden after the last frosts, though in cool summers they grow better in pots in a greenhouse or conservatory.

Many perennial herbs are also easy to grow from seed: fennel, chives and lemon balm, for example, readily self-seed in the garden. With others there may be problems: the seed may be very small or slow to germinate; it may need special conditions like a high temperature, light, or a 'winter' in the freezer!

One particular problem is that shop-bought seed may already be too old: some herb seeds germinate best just after they have ripened. Other herbs – like French tarragon – rarely set seed, and cultivated varieties like the variegated sages and thymes cannot be grown from seed at all.

Unless a lot of one kind of plant is required – to make a hedge or edging, for example – it is often better to buy plants from a garden centre or a specialist herb nursery. Spring is the best time to plant most herbs, though those bought in pots can be put in at any time of year provided that they are well watered.

After-care

The majority of herbs do not need to be cossetted. They are hardy, do not want extra feeding or watering, and are not prone to pest or disease attack. But some do grow quickly, spread easily and have limited lives. It is thus essential to keep the plants in hand and in the best condition for use.

Weeding

They will need regular hoeing and weeding in the first summer after planting – particularly the low, creeping herbs. In subsequent years there should be less space for weeds to grow, but seedlings that

HERBS FOR THE GARDEN (cont.)

Name	Type	Height
LOVAGE	Hardy herbaceous perennial	2 m (6 ft)
MARJORAM (sweet)	Grown as a half-hardy annual	30 cm (1 ft)
MARJORAM (pot) MARJORAM (wild) or oregano	Hardy herbaceous perennials – often difficult to distinguish	38 cm (15 in)
MEADOWSWEET	Hardy herbaceous perennial (native)	60 cm (2 ft)
MINT e.g. applemint, spearmint, gingermint, eau-de-cologne mint, Corsican mint, peppermint	Hardy herbaceous perennials.	Most varieties about 45 cm (18 in). Applemint up to 1 m (3 ft); Corsican mint very low ground cover.
PARSLEY	Bienniel	30 cm (1 ft)
ROSEMARY	Fairly hardy evergreen shrub.	60 cm–1 m (2–3 ft)
SAGE	Hardy evergreen shrub	50 cm (20 in)
SALAD BURNET	Hardy herbaceous perennial	30 cm (1 ft)
SAVORY (summer)	Hardy annual	30 cm (1 ft)
SAVORY (winter)	Hardy shrub – evergreen in mild winters	30 cm (1 ft)
SORREL	Hardy herbaceous perennial	45–75 cm (18–30 in) depending on variety.
SWEET CICELY	Hardy herbaceous perennial	60 cm (2 ft)
TARRAGON	Hardy herbaceous perennial	French tarragon 50 cm (20 in); Russian tarragon 1 m (3 ft)
THYME	Hardy evergreen shrub	Common thyme and other upright varieties 23 cm (9 in); also many creeping forms.

Growing position	Method of growing	Uses
Fairly rich, moist soil; sun or partial shade. Large and not particularly attractive, though can be kept clipped.	From seed best sown indoors in spring, or can divide clumps.	Leaves and seeds have a strong yeasty taste, useful in salads and cooking. Can be dried with care. Flowerheads attract hoverflies.
Light, well-drained soil; sunny, sheltered position, or grows well in pots.	From seed sown in heat in spring.	Spicy leaves used fresh or dried in cooking.
Light, well-drained soil; sunny position. These make good edging herbs; there are attractive golden forms.	From seed sown outdoors or in pots in spring, or can divide clumps.	Mild culinary herbs best used fresh. Oregano is stronger when grown in hot, dry conditions. Good bee plants.
Moist, even boggy soil; sun or partial shade. An attractive poolside plant.	From seed sown in late spring or early autumn, or by division of clumps.	A very useful medicinal herb. Dries well.
Rich, moist soil; partial shade. Some varieties, e.g. gingermint, have attractive foliage, but must be constrained in a flower border. Corsican mint used between paving.	Will grow from pieces of root or can divide clumps (Corsican mint by division only).	Traditional culinary and tea herb; peppermint is of great medicinal value. Dries fairly well and many varieties useful in pot-pourri. All are good bee plants.
Rich, moist soil; partial shade in summer. A good edging herb for flower or vegetable gardens.	From seed sown in spring or late summer – in pots indoors if cold.	An indispensable culinary herb; also has medicinal properties. Best used fresh – from under cloches in winter.
Light, well-drained soil; sunny, sheltered position.	The common variety from seed sown in pots in spring; otherwise buy plants or take cuttings.	A traditional culinary herb; can be used in sweet dishes. Also has useful medicinal properties. Dries well.
Light, well-drained soil; sunny position. Attractive foliage, particularly purple and variegated forms.	The common green variety from seed sown in pots in spring; otherwise best to buy plants or take cuttings.	A traditional culinary herb. Also useful medicinally. Dries well.
Fairly rich, well-drained soil; sunny position. A good edging herb.	From seed sown in the garden or pots in spring. Will self-seed.	Mild culinary herb, best used fresh – keeps in winter.
Light, well-drained soil; sunny position.	From seed sown in the garden or in pots in late spring.	A pungent culinary herb. Dries well.
Light, well-drained soil; sunny position.	From seed sown in pots in late spring.	Used like summer savory, sometimes medicinally.
Fairly rich, moist soil; sun or partial shade.	From seed sown in spring, or can divide clumps.	A sharp culinary herb, best used fresh. Some medicinal properties.
Moist, rich soil; partial shade. An attractive plant in a flower border.	Sow fresh seeds in autumn in the garden – can be difficult to germinate although will self-seed.	A sweet culinary herb. Flowerheads attract hoverflies.
Light, well-drained soil; sunny position. Straggly growth – not particularly attractive plants.	Russian tarragon from seed. French tarragon can be divided, but best to buy plants.	A traditional culinary herb – French tarragon is said to have far superior flavour.
Light, well-drained soil; sunny position. Good edging herbs. Creeping varieties between paving stones and in walls.	Common thyme from seed sown in the garden or pots – will self-seed. Can take cuttings of other thymes or buy plants.	Common thyme and lemon thyme are useful culinary herbs. Common thyme valuable medicinally. All varieties are good bee plants.

have self-sown in the wrong places must be ruthlessly removed. Applying a mulch of well-rotted compost round the lusher types of herb in April will help to control annual weeds, and should also supply the plants with sufficient nutrients. Peat, leafmould or bark could be used round the herbs which prefer poor soils.

Pruning

It is important to trim shrubby herbs to shape every year to prevent them from becoming woody in the centre. There are several periods when this can be done:

● directly after flowering; the plant's energy is not then lost in making seeds and there are no self-sown seedlings to worry about.

● some time between flowering and early September; this should allow the seed of early flowering herbs to be collected or left to attract birds (finches are very fond of sage seed, for example). Do not prune later than this, otherwise frost may damage young growth subsequently produced and cause older branches to die back.

● at the end of March or in early April; this is the best time to do any drastic pruning involving cutting into the old wood; you do, however, risk loosing the blooms of early flowering herbs for that year.

Most herbaceous herbs need cutting back some time after mid summer if fresh young shoots are to grow. But of course this means there will be no flowers or seed produced. A good compromise is to clip the straggling growth round the edge of the clump and leave the centre to bloom. Tall clumps may need staking. Dead growth should either be removed in late autumn after the first few frosts or left until early spring to provide some protection for the crowns of the plants.

Winter care

Most perennial herbs overwinter with no prob-

lems if planted in the right place – waterlogging can do more harm than cold. Rosemary and lemon thyme are more tender than most of the hardy shrubs and should be cloched during the worst of the weather while they are small. French tarragon is sometimes difficult to establish, and mulching the crown with straw in late autumn may help.

Some salad herbs will grow under cloches throughout mild spells in winter, providing welcome greenery. Examples are chervil and rocket (both sown in late summer), parsley and salad burnet.

Pests and diseases

With their reputation for keeping other plants free of pests and diseases it is hardly surprising that herbs suffer few problems themselves. The soft growth of young plants may be attacked by aphids – particularly when they are being started off indoors. The best remedy is to pinch out the tips of the shoots where the aphids congregate (this is necessary anyway for producing bushy plants). Then try insecticidal soap, derris or quassia (see page 36). Another possible problem is carrot root fly – producing yellowing or wilting leaves on parsley and any other herb in the Umbelliferae family. However, attacks should be rare when the herbs are among other plants, and strong perennial plants should anyway recover by themselves. Parsley may have to be dug up and burned.

Both mint and comfrey can suffer from rust disease. With mint, this can be cured by burning off the dead foliage in autumn. Comfrey rust is not so easily dealt with: the best answer is to keep the plant growing strongly and to cut it often.

Replacing plants

Many herbs deteriorate rapidly after three or four years, so you should be prepared to renew them. Clumps of herbaceous herbs like tarragon, mints and lovage should be lifted and divided after this time like ornamental perennials (see page 106). Take the opportunity to work well-rooted compost into the soil before replanting. Regular division like this is also the best way to keep vigorous plants in check.

Angelica plants rarely survive for more than five years, so in this case one or two self-sown seedlings can be allowed to grow on in preparation.

Shrubby herbs like thyme and sage tend to become straggly and woody in the centre, so it is a good policy to propagate a few young plants and gradually replace them: these will look better, be less subject to disease and have more flavour.

Harvesting and preserving

Fresh sprigs of herbs picked straight from the garden undoubtedly have the best flavour and most therapeutic value. However, those that you harvest carefully and dry or freeze at home for winter use can be far superior to the shop-bought products. The range of these is anyway limited, and there is no guarantee that chemicals have not been used to grow them.

Timing the harvest

Once plants are established, leaves can be picked for use throughout the growing season. However, at some point they will be at their peak – that is, the aromatic oils will be most concentrated – and this is the ideal time to harvest leaves for drying or freezing. Often the peak occurs just before the plant flowers, so use this as a guide. The leaves of herbaceous herbs are obviously not in good condition in autumn just before they die, and those of evergreen herbs have little flavour in mid

A 'chequer-board' herb garden is not only decorative but facilitates gathering in wet weather

winter. The weather also makes a difference to the harvest: there is most oil in the leaves on a sunny morning after the dew has dried but before the sun gets too hot.

Roots, on the other hand, are best harvested in winter when the plant is dormant and the leaves have returned all nutrients to them for storage. Seeds must be fully ripe – ideally left on the plant until they are about to drop naturally. In wet or windy weather the whole seedheads should be cut off as they begin to turn, and hung up somewhere warm, dry and airy to finish ripening.

Drying and storing

Drying herb leaves successfully is very much a matter of experience. Individual herbs dry best under different conditions and take different lengths of time. All dried herbs should be stored in airtight containers. These should be opaque or be put in a dark cupboard as light causes the herbs to deteriorate in quality.

The methods are a compromise: the herbs must be dried as quickly as possible so that they do not go musty, but on the other hand the temperature must not be too high or the plant tissues are damaged and the essential oils escape. The most difficult herbs to dry are thus the delicate succulent herbs like parsley, chervil, chives, tarragon and basil, whereas those with dry, small leaves like thyme and rosemary retain their flavour well. Herb flowers which are also delicate are dried in the same way.

The essential conditions are darkness, air and warmth – a temperature of 21–23°C (70–90°F). The airing cupboard or the warming drawer of an oven with the door left ajar are both suitable places for small quantities. An attic or shed may do during the summer. Hang the herbs in bunches or spread them out in thin layers on paper. Delicate herbs should only take about three days to become brittle and rustle to the touch, whereas tough, thick leaves will take more like two weeks.

Roots and seeds are less temperamental to dry than leaves and flowers. Roots should be cut into small pieces and dried at a slightly higher tempera-

ture – a very low oven can be used. Seedheads should be dried off naturally for two or three weeks in a sunny or warm, airy place.

If freezer space is limited it should be kept for the delicate herbs mentioned earlier, which do not dry well. They can simply be frozen in sprigs put into small polythene bags – there is no need to blanch them.

Using herbs

Herbs in the kitchen

Everybody knows that parsley can be used as a garnish, sage in stuffing and mint in sauce. But herbs need not be confined to such familiar roles: they can be used in soups, salads, bread and biscuits, and even in jam, wine and sweet dishes. Fresh or dried herbs can enhance almost any meal – from a quick snack to a dinner party.

Which herbs and what quantities to use is largely a matter of individual taste. As we have seen, the strength of fresh herbs can depend on the time of year and how they are grown, and the quality of dried herbs is even more variable. However, a few general guidelines on the suitability of various herbs can be given as a basis for experiment.

The first factor to consider is not so much the taste of the herb leaves but their texture. Those with hard, dry leaves like thyme, rosemary, sage and bay are obviously not suitable for using raw in salads or as a garnish. They do not break down quickly and are best added to dishes during cooking: they then have time gradually to impart their flavour.

Herbs with succulent leaves are usually good in salads – used lavishly if they are mild-flavoured (like parsley, sorrel and salad burnet) but sparingly, usually in specific dishes, if they have strong, distinctive flavours (basil with tomatoes and dill with cucumber, for example). Flowers, like those of the nasturtium, are often used to add colour. In hot dishes the delicate herbs are best added only just before the end of cooking or as a garnish. They are useful for quickly cooked egg and cheese dishes – the *fines herbes* traditional in omelettes consists of chopped parsley, chervil, tarragon and chives.

The strength of any herb not only determines how much of it is used but also which herbs can be combined with it. The mild herbs like parsley and chervil seem to enhance the flavour of any herb with which they are mixed, but the really pungent herbs should not be put together in one dish. Herb seeds are concentrated sources of flavour – but use only those that are recommended for cooking like caraway, lovage, fennel and dill because the very strength of some others can make them harmful.

Herbs for home remedies

Many of the culinary herbs have therapeutic properties. Eating small amounts of them regularly will help to maintain health, and some can be used as more specific remedies. Other useful medicinal herbs are found among common garden weeds – yarrow and ribwort plantain, for example. Thus only a few need to be grown specially to make up a useful medicine chest.

They should not, however, be regarded as substitutes for drugs. The principle of herbal remedies is that they help the body to help itself, working alongside the natural healing processes rather than suppressing symptoms like chemical medicines. As such they are wonderfully effective – all the various constituents of a herb working together to bring about a true cure without any of the side effects of some modern medicines.

You should of course only use herbs to treat minor ailments, and if you are unsure of the symptoms or the identification of the herb you should seek expert help.

The most convenient way to take a herbal medicine is in the form of a tea, made by adding boiling water to dried or fresh herbs in a cup or pot. The strength usually recommended is 30 g to 500 ml (1 oz to 1 pt), though, as with culinary herbs, to prescribe exact quantities is not very meaningful. Some herbs should not be taken over an extended period or by those with other medical conditions, so always check any unusual remedy with a good herbal.

Most herbs, however, are completely safe and often make pleasant drinks as alternatives to tea and coffee: the mild relaxing herbs like lemon balm and chamomile, for example, or the mints, which are gentle aids to digestion. Other useful remedies include fennel and dill for stomach pains, and yarrow and elderflower for feverish colds; thyme, sage and garlic have an antiseptic action, useful both in cases of flu and for stomach upsets.

Some herbs can also be used externally, made into a poultice or an ointment. Comfrey, for example, has a deserved reputation for healing cuts, bruises and strains, and pot marigolds for soothing skin inflammation.

Herbs in pot-pourri

Dried herbs can have more than just practical value – a pot-pourri to put in bowls around the house is easy to make from the garden and carries with it lasting memories of the plants and flowers.

A simple pot-pourri is just a mixture of scented leaves and colourful flowers, dried as described on page 124, though sometimes spices and concentrated oils are added. It also contains a fixative – usually orris – to help it keep its fragrance.

As with herb cookery, there is no need for fixed 'recipes'. Herbs with definable perfumes like lavender, eau-de-cologne mint and many of the scented geraniums are a good base for a mixture, but any of the sweet or spicy herbs, like sweet marjoram, rosemary and basil, blend in well. The flowers of bergamot, pinks and roses add colour as well as fragrance.

FURTHER READING

Baines, Chris *How to make a Wildlife Garden* (Elm Tree Books, 1985)

Baker, Harry *Fruit* (Mitchell Beazley, 1980)

Chinery, Michael *Garden Creepy Crawlies* (Whittet Books, 1986)

Hills, Lawrence *The Good Fruit Guide* (Henry Doubleday Research Association, 1984)

Kitto, Dick *Composting: The Cheap and Natural Way to Make Your Garden Grow.* (Thorsons, 1984)

Larkcom, Joy *The Salad Garden* (Windward, 1984)

Larkcom, Joy *Vegetables from Small Gardens* (Faber & Faber, 1986)

Owen, Jennifer *Garden Life* (Chatto & Windus 1983)

Pears, Pauline *Raised Bed Gardening the Organic Way* (Henry Doubleday Research Association, 1983)

Salter, P., Bleasdale, J. *et al. Know and Grow Vegetables* (Oxford University Press, Book 1 1979, Book 2 1982)

Stickland, Sue *Planning the Organic Flower Garden* (Thorsons, 1986)

Stickland, Sue *Planning the Organic Herb Garden* (Thorsons, 1986)

Turner, David and Muir, Ken *The Handbook of Soft Fruit Growing* (Croom Helm, 1985)

INDEX

Page numbers in italics indicate illustrations